PATCHWORK MATH 1

100
ADDITION AND SUBTRACTION REPRODUCIBLES
DEBRA BAYCURA

SCHOLASTIC
PROFESSIONAL BOOKS

New York ■ Toronto ■ London ■ Auckland ■ Sydney

To Mike, Cara and Mikey.

Design and illustrations by Peter Samek.

Cover design by Vincent Ceci.

ISBN 0-590-49073-7

12 11 10 9 8   0 1 2 3 4 5/9
                                                        31

Printed in the U.S.A.

About the Author

Graule Studio

Debra Baycura has been an elementary school teacher for 15 years. She studied at Indiana University of Pennsylvania and Slippery Rock University, and is currently working on an Elementary Principal Certificate at Westminster College.

Debra lives with her husband and three children in New Brighton, Pennsylvania. She says, "Although I have never made a quilt, the designs and history of American quilts fascinate me."

Contents

Contents

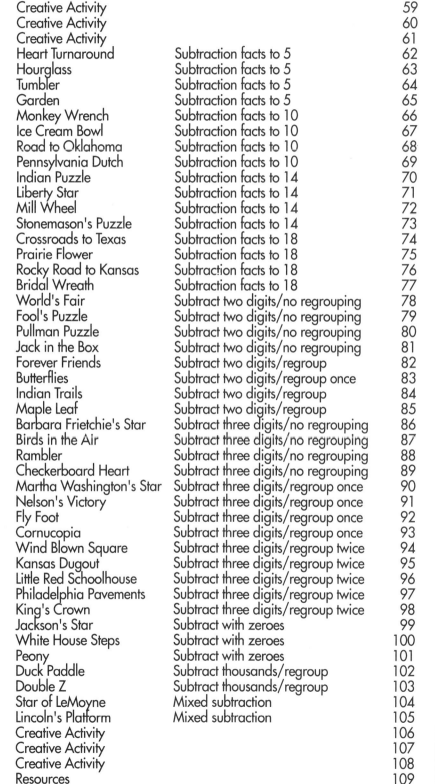

Introduction

About the Book

■ This skills book provides you with worksheets to reinforce addition and subtraction skills.

■ It also introduces historical background about the name of each quilt design. Each design is an authentic American pattern. Further investigation of the historical period or personage will develop and refine your students' inquiry skills.

■ The Contents page lists each design and the math function it reinforces. The skills are arranged in progressive level of difficulty.

■ Directions for the student have been kept to a minimum to ensure easy use by students of all ability levels.

■ The CHALLENGE (*C*) activity at the bottom of each page is an extension activity that involves language arts, social studies, or math.

■ The creative activities on pages 59–61 and 106–108 allow students to design and name their own quilt patterns. You may want to mount the shape manipulatives on oak tag and keep them for future use.

Class Activities

■ Your students may want to save their completed pages and arrange them on a wall or bulletin board to make a big class quilt.

■ Students can use the shape manipulatives on the creative activity pages to cut patchwork shapes from construction paper or wrapping paper and piece them together to make a quilt square. Several of these quilt squares will make a colorful wall or bulletin board border.

■ Your students may be interested to know that people in many parts of the country still design and make quilts. Your class could choose a hero, a local tree or flower, a national monument, or an important class celebration and design and color a quilt.

A Short History of Quilting

Quilting is the sewing together of two or three thicknesses of cloth. People throughout history have quilted cloth. Quilting has always served two purposes. Some people quilt to make warm clothing or bed covers. Others quilt to create works of art.

For centuries, people in China have quilted cloth for warm winter clothing. In the Middle Ages, the Crusaders liked to wear quilted shirts to prevent chafing under their heavy chain mail. Queens quilted and peasant women quilted. Many designs were passed down from generation to generation.

Quilting was introduced to the New World when Pilgrims traveled across the ocean on the Mayflower. When the coverlets and quilts they brought from England wore out, the Pilgrims mended them with strong pieces of material from worn-out clothing and blankets. These scrap quilts, considered the first crazy quilts, were probobly not beautiful but were very functional.

Naming quilt designs is a custom as old as quilt making itself. Some names reflect contemporary slang, popular sayings, and political activities and customs. Some quilts were named for tools and machines. In other designs you can see trees or flowers or religious symbols.

Many of the quilt designs in this book have more than one name. That is because people all over the country make quilts. The histories given for each quilt name are as close to accurate as possible. When there was a choice of name for the quilt, the one that would most appeal to students was chosen.

Cowboy's Star

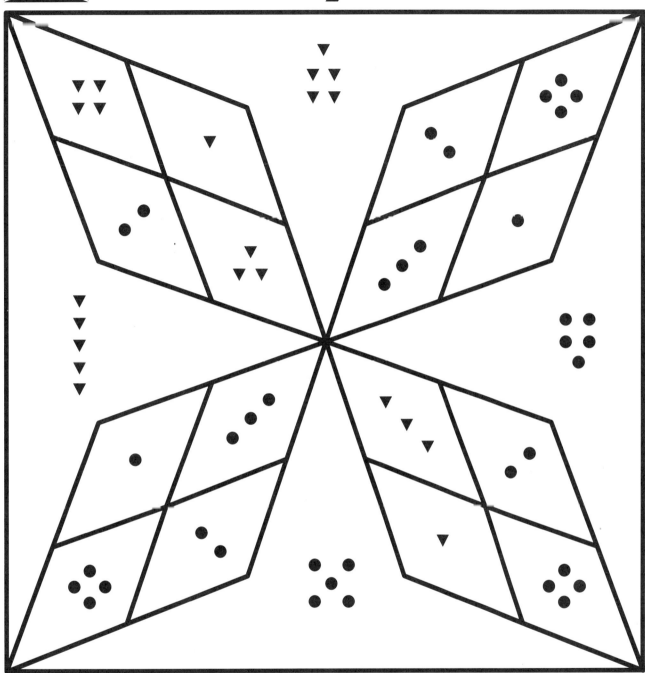

Color:
  1 = blue
  2 = blue
  3 = red
  4 = green
  5 = orange

America's past was honored by naming this picture for the cowboys who roamed the West.

C Roll a dice five times. On the back of this sheet of paper, write the number for each roll.

9

Pinwheel

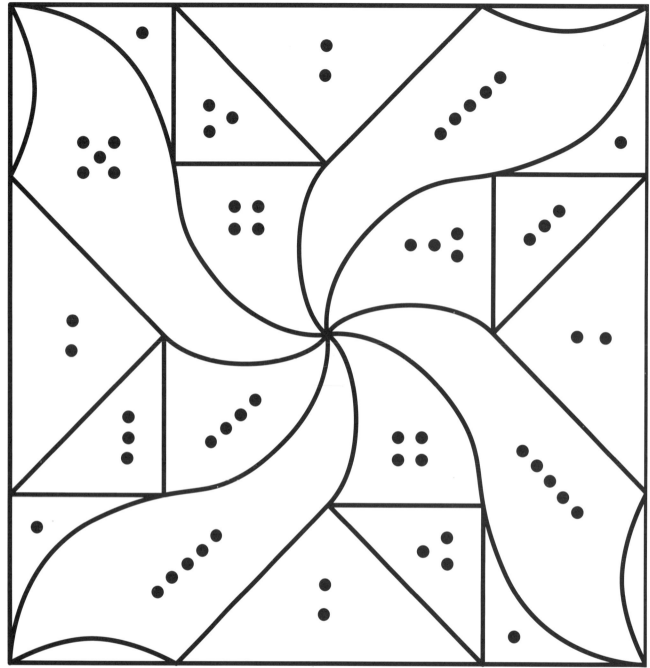

Color:

   1 = green
   2 = blue
   3 = yellow
   4 = green
   5 = red

Can you see the pinwheel shape in this picture?

C Use three colors to draw your favorite toy on the back of this sheet of paper.

The Basket

Color:

6 = yellow
7 = green
8 = brown
9 = red
10 = green

In colonial times people used baskets to carry things. They couldn't use paper bags because bags were not invented yet.

C On the back of this sheet of paper, draw a basket filled with six things you would carry in it.

Brown Goose

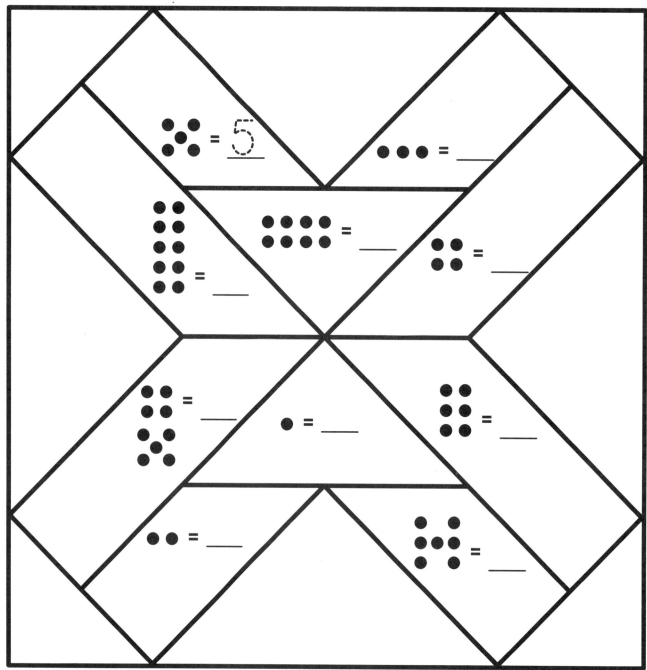

Color:

2 and 3 = blue
5 and 7 = green
1 and 8 = yellow
4, 6, 9, and 10 = brown

Long ago, Mrs. Brown loved her pet goose so much she named her new quilt picture after him.

C Draw a picture of your pet on the back of this sheet of paper.

Flowers in a Pot

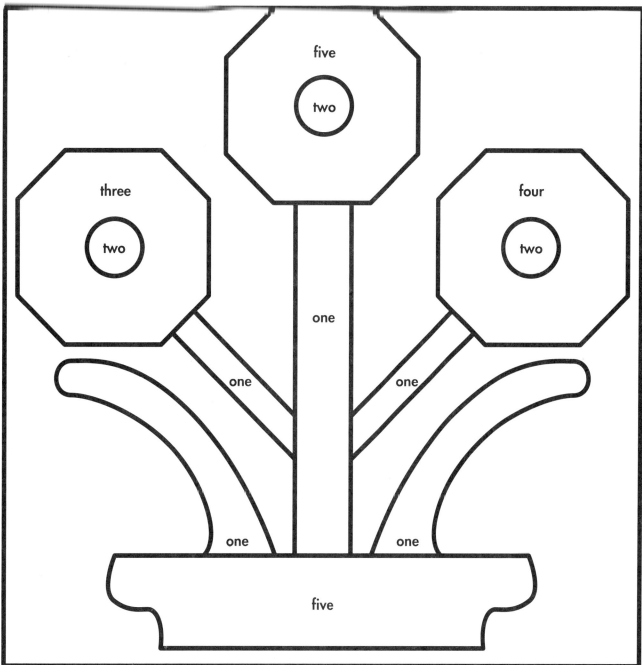

Count the dots in the boxes. Then color the matching number word.

⚀ = green

⚁ = yellow

⚂ = red

⚃ = purple

⚄ = blue

It is always nice to see pretty flowers in a pot.

C Use bright colors to draw a pot of flowers on the back of this sheet of paper.

Sunbonnet Sue

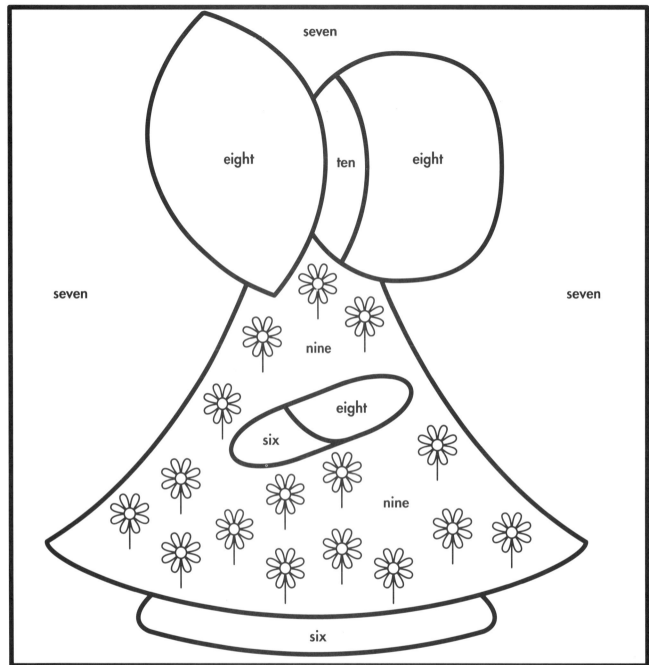

Count the dots in the boxes. Then color the matching number word.

⚅ = black ⚄ = orange

⚄ = green ⚅ = yellow

⚅ = red

Many young children wanted a "Sunbonnet Sue" quilt to keep them warm.

C Roll two dice. On the back of this sheet of paper, write the number of the sum you roll.

14

Butterfly

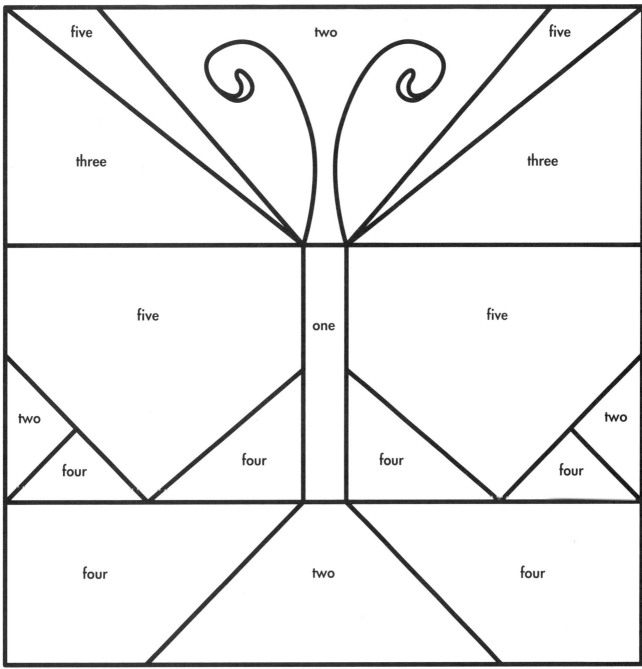

Color:
1 = black
2 = blue
3 = yellow
4 = brown
5 = orange

Colorful butterflies flutter past on sunny days.

C Draw five butterflies on the back of this sheet of paper. On each butterfly, write one number word. Use the words for 1, 2, 3, 4, and 5.

Koala Blue

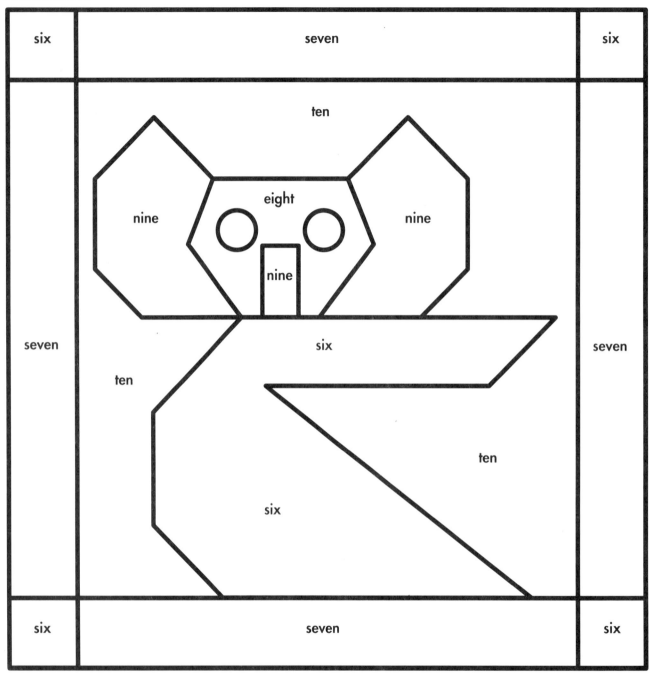

six	seven	six

ten

nine   eight   nine

nine

seven   six   seven

ten

ten

six

six	seven	six

Color:

6 = blue
7 = red
8 = brown
9 = black
10 = yellow

This cute little bear lives in Australia.

C Make five cards. Write the number word for 6, 7, 8, 9, and 10 on a card. Practice at home.

Moon and Stars

Color:
3 = white
4 = blue
5 = yellow

Can you see the moon and stars from your bedroom window? Try to see them tonight!

C After this page has been checked, put each of the problems on a star-shaped flashcard. Practice the problems tonight.

Fish Pond

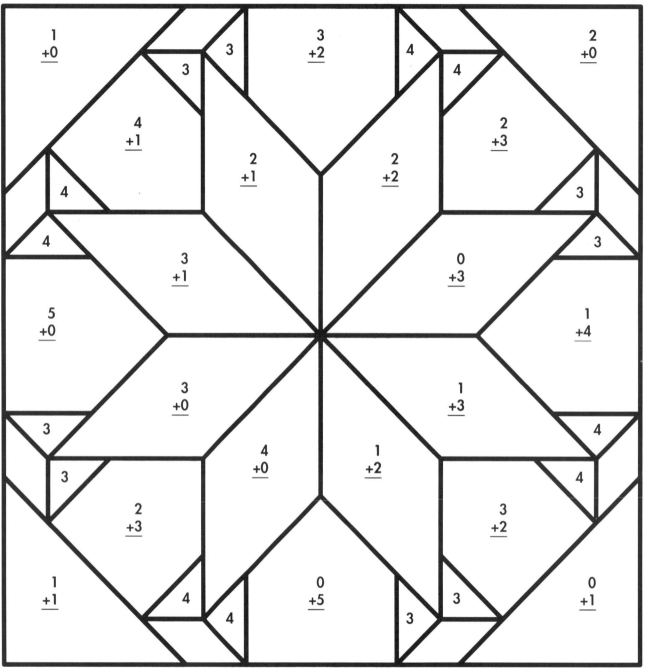

Color:
1 and 2 = green
    3 = yellow
    4 = orange
    5 = blue

Here is your very own goldfish pond and you don't even have to feed the fish.

C Write the facts for 4 and 5 on goldfish-shaped flashcards. Put the fish in a "pond" between you and a friend. Take turns "fishing" for cards, keeping the ones you answer correctly. The person with the most cards at the end is the winner.

Streak of Lightning

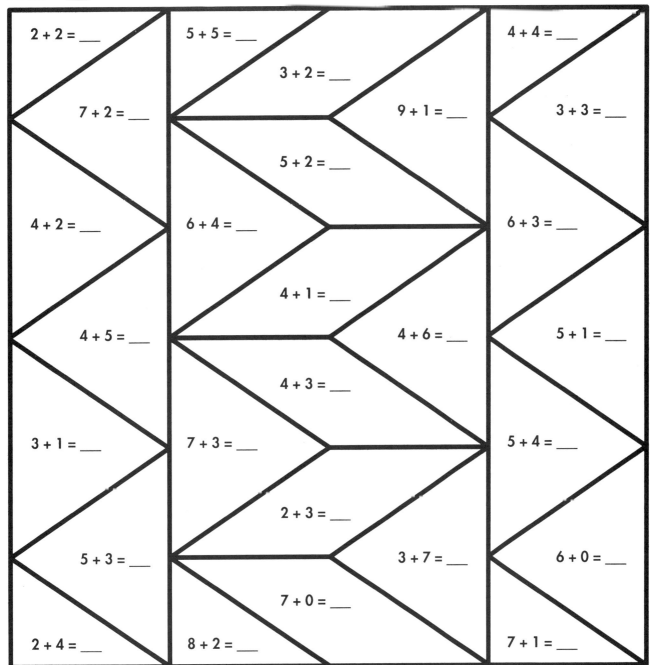

Color:
4 and 6 = yellow
5 and 7 = orange
8 and 9 = green
        10 = purple

Have you ever seen lightning streak across the sky?

_____

C Tell what you should do to be safe in a lightning storm.

19

Red Cross

5 +3	3 +4	6 +1	2 +6
4 +5	5 +5	6 +4	5 +4
8 +2	2 +1	2 +7	3 +7
5 +2	4 +4	7 +0	4 +3

3 +3

| 2 +4 | 6 +0 | 4 +2 |

3 +5	2 +5	8 +0	6 +2
7 +3	7 +2	3 +6	4 +6
1 +8	2 +8	9 +1	8 +1
0 +8	7 +1	3 +4	1 +6

5 +1

Color:
- 6 = red
- 7 = yellow
- 8 = yellow
- 9 = blue
- 10 = orange

This picture honors the Red Cross, an international group that helps people who get sick or hurt in time of war or disaster.

C Find a hospital sign in a magazine, book, or on a street sign. Report where you found it.

Chicago Star

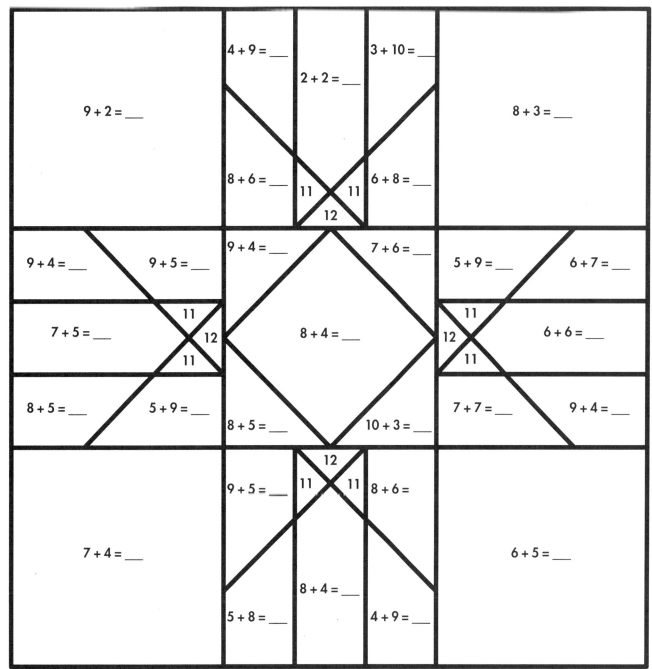

$9 + 2 = \_\_$

$4 + 9 = \_\_$

$2 + 2 = \_\_$

$3 + 10 = \_\_$

$8 + 3 = \_\_$

$8 + 6 = \_\_$ 11   11 $6 + 8 = \_\_$

12

$9 + 4 = \_\_$ $9 + 5 = \_\_$ $9 + 4 = \_\_$ $7 + 6 = \_\_$ $5 + 9 = \_\_$ $6 + 7 = \_\_$

11   11

$7 + 5 = \_\_$ 12 $8 + 4 = \_\_$ 12 $6 + 6 = \_\_$

11   11

$8 + 5 = \_\_$ $5 + 9 = \_\_$ $7 + 7 = \_\_$ $9 + 4 = \_\_$

$8 + 5 = \_\_$ $10 + 3 = \_\_$

12

$9 + 5 = \_\_$ 11   11 $8 + 6 = \_\_$

$7 + 4 = \_\_$ $6 + 5 = \_\_$

$8 + 4 = \_\_$

$5 + 8 = \_\_$ $4 + 9 = \_\_$

Color:
  11 = green
  12 = orange
  13 = blue
  14 = red

The city of Chicago is honored
in this square.

_____

C On the back of this sheet of paper, write
the names of three cities that you know.

Wedding Ring

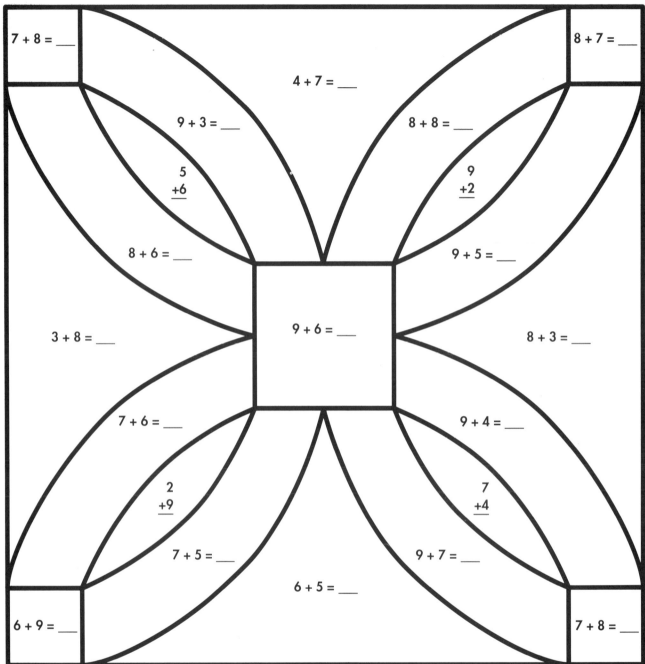

7 + 8 = ___

8 + 7 = ___

4 + 7 = ___

9 + 3 = ___

8 + 8 = ___

$\begin{array}{r} 5 \\ +6 \\ \hline \end{array}$

$\begin{array}{r} 9 \\ +2 \\ \hline \end{array}$

8 + 6 = ___

9 + 5 = ___

3 + 8 = ___

9 + 6 = ___

8 + 3 = ___

7 + 6 = ___

9 + 4 = ___

$\begin{array}{r} 2 \\ +9 \\ \hline \end{array}$

$\begin{array}{r} 7 \\ +4 \\ \hline \end{array}$

7 + 5 = ___

9 + 7 = ___

6 + 5 = ___

6 + 9 = ___

7 + 8 = ___

Color:
- 11 = purple
- 12 = orange
- 13 = green
- 14 = blue
- 15 = yellow
- 16 = red

This design was used on quilts for couples who were going to get married. Can you see half-circles that could form a wedding ring?

C Count as many circles as you can see in your classroom. On the back of this sheet of paper, make an addition problem for that amount.

Broken Dishes

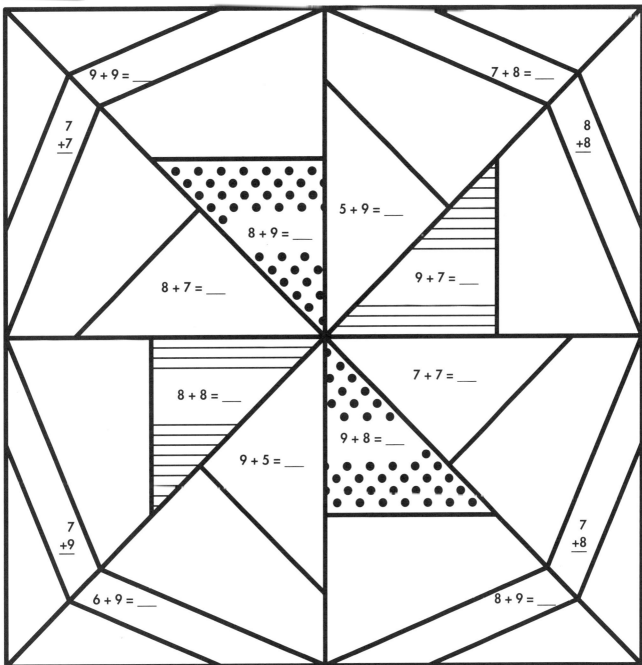

9 + 9 = ___

7
+7

7 + 8 = ___

8
+8

5 + 9 = ___

8 + 9 = ___

8 + 7 = ___

9 + 7 = ___

8 + 8 = ___

7 + 7 = ___

9 + 5 = ___

9 + 8 = ___

7
+9

7
+8

6 + 9 = ___

8 + 9 = ___

Color:
14 and 15 = yellow
        16 = blue
17 and 18 = red

Putting these broken dishes back together would be a very difficult job.

C When you complete the math, cut out the eight triangles in the center. Glue these "broken dishes" together again on another sheet of paper.

Album

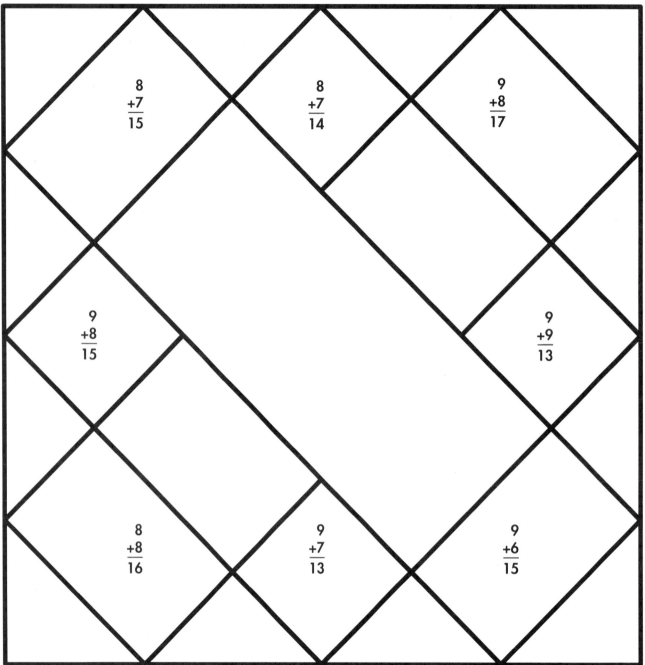

$$\begin{array}{r} 8 \\ +7 \\ \hline 15 \end{array} \qquad \begin{array}{r} 8 \\ +7 \\ \hline 14 \end{array} \qquad \begin{array}{r} 9 \\ +8 \\ \hline 17 \end{array}$$

$$\begin{array}{r} 9 \\ +8 \\ \hline 15 \end{array} \qquad \qquad \begin{array}{r} 9 \\ +9 \\ \hline 13 \end{array}$$

$$\begin{array}{r} 8 \\ +8 \\ \hline 16 \end{array} \qquad \begin{array}{r} 9 \\ +7 \\ \hline 13 \end{array} \qquad \begin{array}{r} 9 \\ +6 \\ \hline 15 \end{array}$$

Color:

If the answer is correct, color it blue.

If the answer is wrong, color it red.

The "Album" quilt was a gift for the bride-to-be. Each friend would quilt a square and sew her name in the middle of it. Then all the friends would combine the squares into an "Album" quilt.

C Make and sign your own "Album" quilt squares to display for the school.

Chinese Puzzle

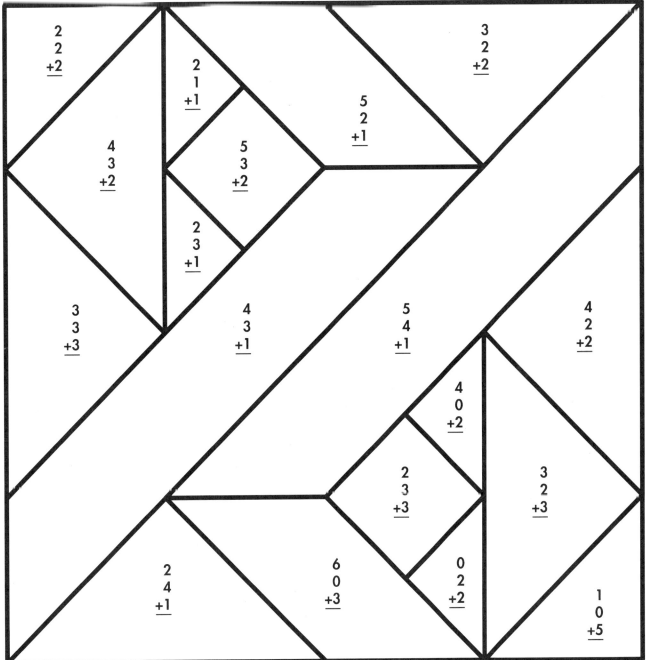

Color:

4 and 6 = red

7 = orange

8 = yellow

9 and 10 = blue

To protect their faces from the sun and rain, the Chinese people used to wear triangle-shaped hats. How many triangles can you find in this square?

C Find names of two other countries in the newspaper, and write them on the back of this sheet of paper.

Weathervane

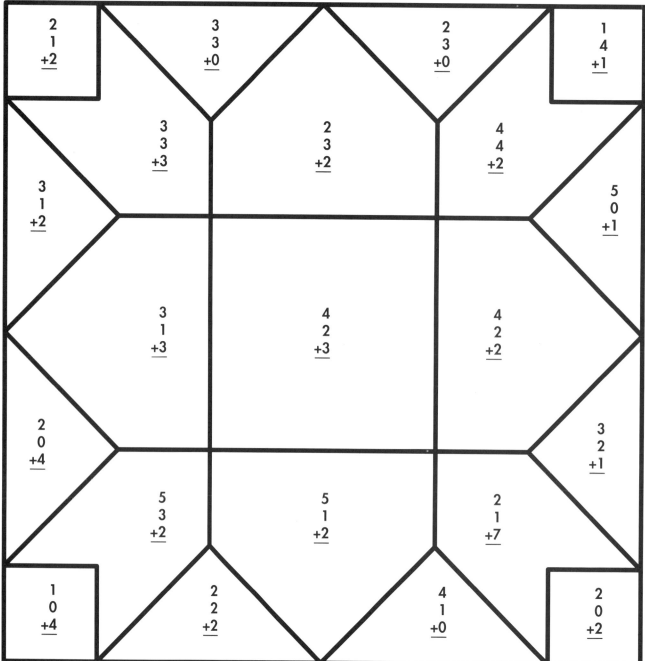

Color:
4, 5, and 6 = green
  7 and 8 = yellow
  9 and 10 = red

Great-Grandma used to predict the weather with a weathervane. Why? There were no TVs or radios, of course!

C On the back of this sheet of paper, draw a weathervane you have seen.

Cupid's Arrowpoint

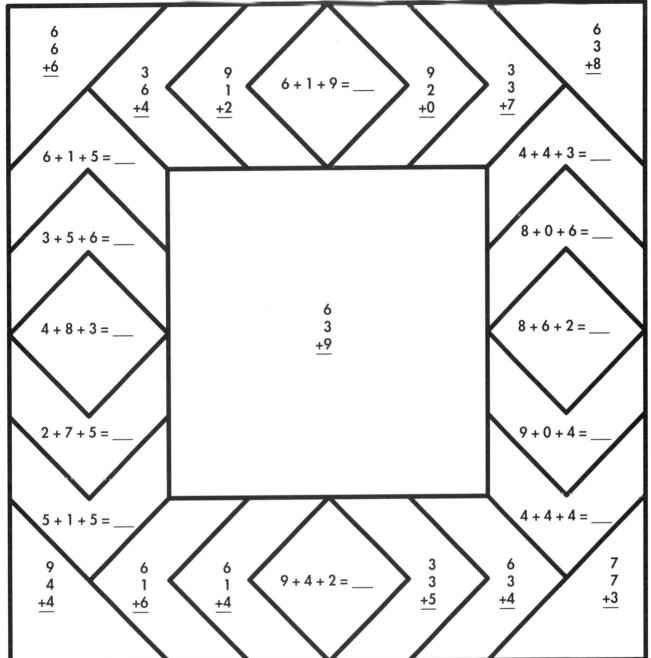

6
6
+6

3
6
+4

9
1
+2

6 + 1 + 9 = ___

9
2
+0

3
3
+7

6
3
+8

6 + 1 + 5 = ___

4 + 4 + 3 = ___

3 + 5 + 6 = ___

8 + 0 + 6 = ___

4 + 8 + 3 = ___

6
3
+9

8 + 6 + 2 = ___

2 + 7 + 5 = ___

9 + 0 + 4 = ___

5 + 1 + 5 = ___

4 + 4 + 4 = ___

9
4
+4

6
1
+6

6
1
+4

9 + 4 + 2 = ___

3
3
+5

6
3
+4

7
7
+3

Color:

11 and 12 = red

13 and 14 = green

15 and 16 = blue

17 and 18 = yellow

This design honored love and romance. Although you can't see any arrows in this picture, there are many, many points.

C Make a Valentine for a friend.

Churn Dash

```
 6          7          5
 5          7          2
+3         +1         +7
```

```
 5          9          3
 3          6          4
+9         +3         +9
```

```
 6     4        8        0      4
 2     5        0        9      5
+6    +9       +8       +9     +5
```

```
 6          8          8
 3          1          0
+7         +9         +9
```

```
 6                                7
 3              8                 2
+6              6                +6
               +0
```

Color:

14 and 15 = red
16 and 17 = blue
18 = brown

This is a picture of an old butter churn—
the kind Great-Grandma used to make
butter every week.

C On the back of this sheet of paper, make a list
of five ways you use butter at your house.

28

Oriole Window

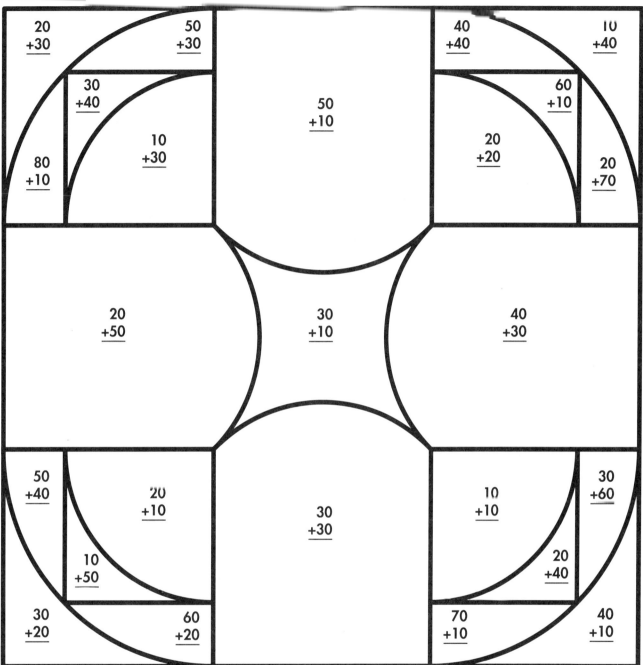

Color:

20, 30, and 40 = red

50 = green

60 and 70 = blue

80 = orange

90 = yellow

Many houses, old and new, have windows made with many pieces of colored glass.

C On the back of this sheet of paper, use pieces of colored paper to make an Oriole window.

Orange Peel

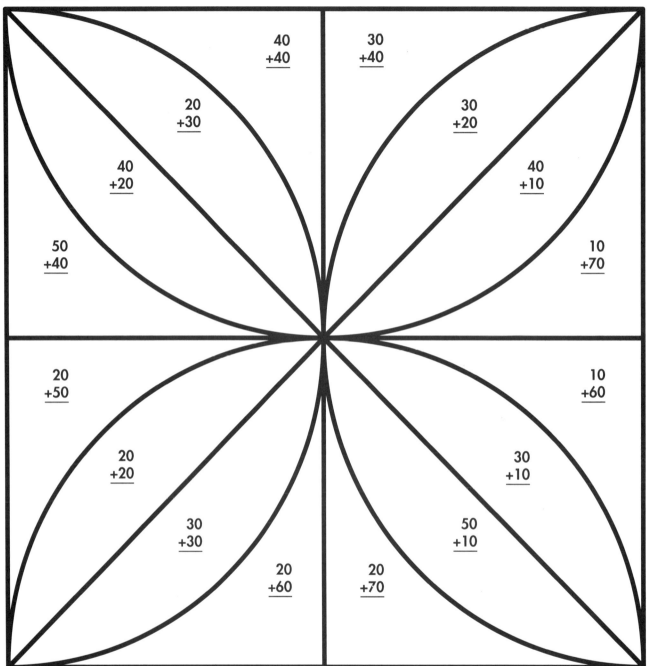

Color:

40, 50, and 60 = orange
70, 80, and 90 = green

A young girl received a piece of fruit as a party favor. She never wanted to forget this treasure. She sewed a picture of the peels into a quilt.

C On the back of this sheet of paper, list five fruits you like in A-B-C order.

Wild Goose Chase

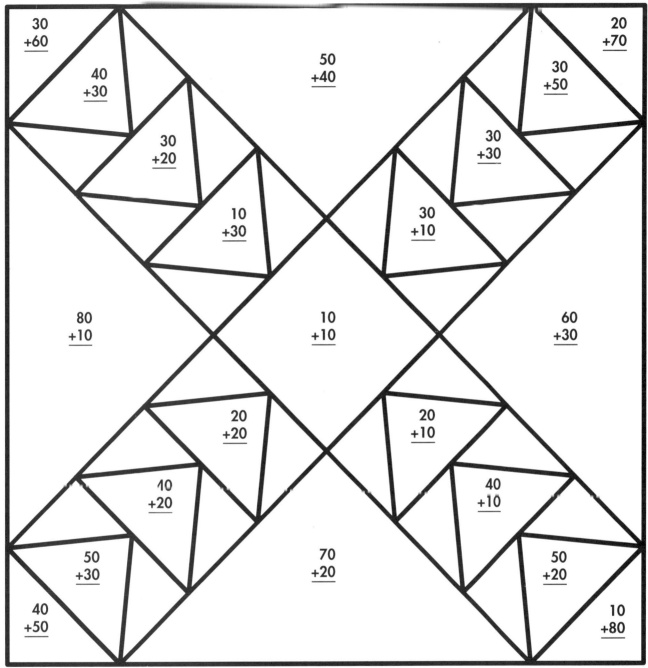

Color:

20 = yellow
30 and 40 = purple
50 and 60 = orange
70 and 80 = green
90 = red

Can you see the "V" pattern geese make when they fly in a group?

C Put three of these problems on flashcards. Practice them with a friend.

Space Station

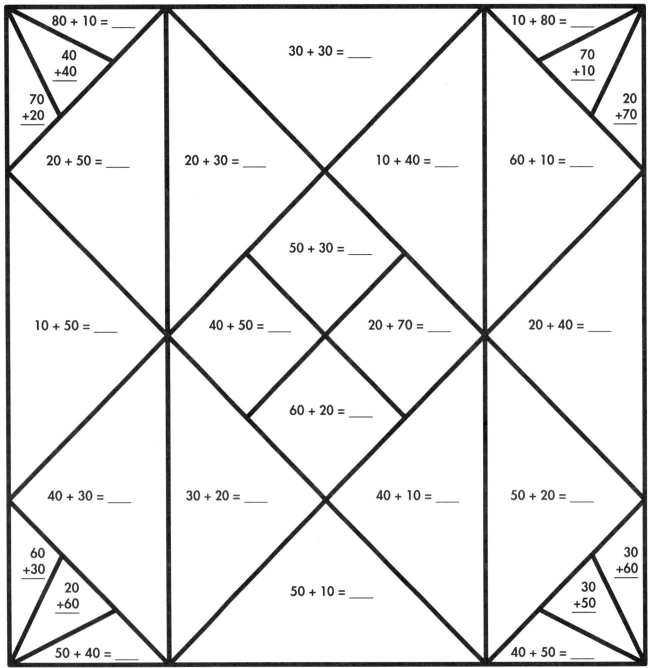

80 + 10 = ___

40
+40

70
+20

20 + 50 = ___

10 + 50 = ___

40 + 30 = ___

60
+30

20
+60

50 + 40 = ___

30 + 30 = ___

20 + 30 = ___

50 + 30 = ___

40 + 50 = ___

20 + 70 = ___

60 + 20 = ___

30 + 20 = ___

50 + 10 = ___

10 + 80 = ___

70
+10

20
+70

10 + 40 = ___

60 + 10 = ___

20 + 40 = ___

40 + 10 = ___

50 + 20 = ___

30
+60

30
+50

40 + 50 = ___

Color:

50 = green
60 = white
70 = red
80 = yellow
90 = blue

This picture honors America's adventures in space.

C On the back of this sheet of paper, write five facts for the sum of 90.

The Rolling Stone

82 +15	37 +41	23 +15
52 +41		
37 +41	32 +13	32 +23

63 +14	19 +60
12 +11	
15 +40	34 +13

13 +23	39 +20	31 +10	44 +10	13 +20

42 +36	50 +45	28 +31
43 +20		
38 +41	43 +24	19 +20

16 +42	70 +17
30 +13	
19 +60	35 +62

Color:

If the answer has a 5, color blue.

If the answer has a 3, color orange.

If the answer has a 1, color yellow.

If the answer has a 7, color red.

This design looks as if it could roll away from you. It is often called "The Wheel." What makes you think it looks like a rolling stone?

C Find five pictures of things that have wheels. Paste the pictures on the back of this sheet of paper.

Sunflower Star

32
+24

16
+40

77
+12

54
+14

34
+34

53
+36

26
+63

23
+45

35
+62

38
+30

22
+67

47
+42

51
+17

46
+22

71
+18

33
+23

44
+12

Color:

56 = green

68 = orange

89 = yellow

97 = blue

In the winter, when everything outside was white with snow, the pioneer women loved making this design because of its bright colors.

C Write your age on four flashcards, and then add a 6, 7, 8, and 9 to each of the cards. Practice the facts with a friend.

34

Shoo-Fly

41 +43 33 +31	60 +21	52 +21	85 +11 24 +34
43 +30	32 +24	32 +32	52 +27
41 +40	14 +44	46 +10	42 +31
30 +34 53 +43	51 +30	43 +36	33 +25 22 +62

Color:
56, 58, and 64 = black
73, 79, and 81 = red
        84, and 96 = green

The Amish people make a pie called a Shoo-Fly pie. (What would you say if a fly were buzzing around your fresh-baked pie? SHOO-FLY!)

C On the back of this sheet of paper, make three problems that add up to 67.

Skyrocket

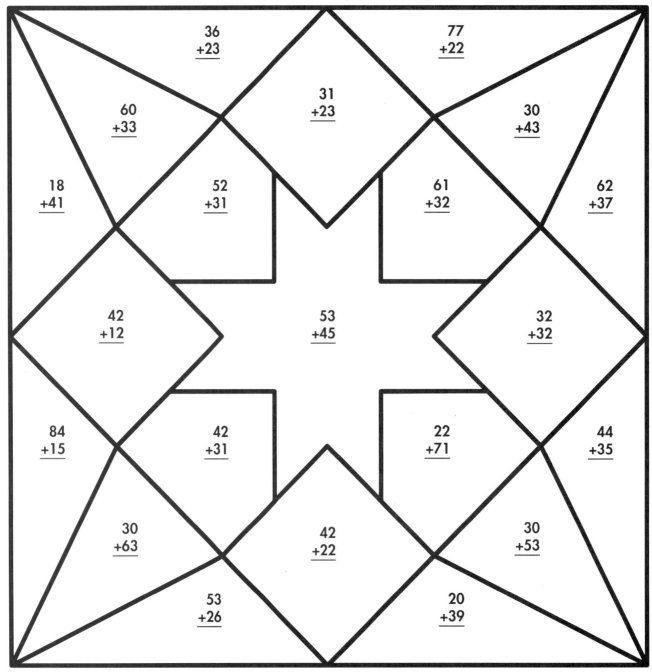

Color:

54 and 64 = yellow

59, 79, and 99 = blue

73, 83, and 93 = black

98 = green

Can you see the rockets flying into the sky?

C On the back of this sheet of paper, draw a rocket blasting off to outer space.

Crazy Quilt

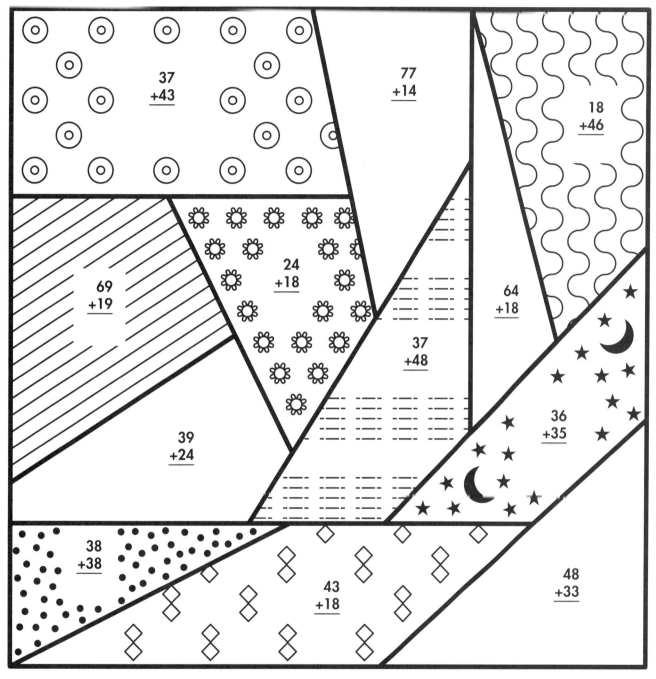

Cross out each answer in the number bank as you complete each problem. Use your favorite colors to complete the picture.

Great-Grandma used scraps of material and old clothing to make this quilt. It sure did look "crazy" when it was finished!

42	61	63	64	71	76
80	81	82	85	88	91

C Design your own crazy quilt on a larger sheet of paper. Use designs from clothes you have.

State of Ohio

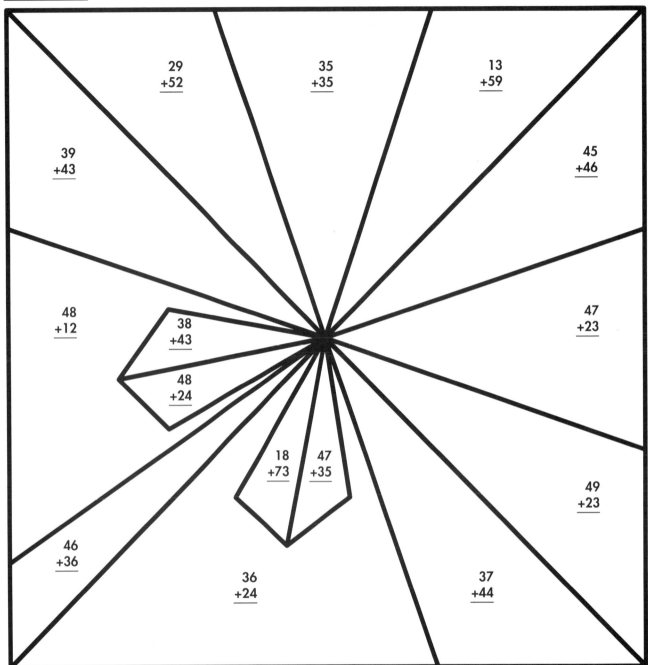

29
+52

35
+35

13
+59

39
+43

45
+46

48
+12

38
+43

47
+23

48
+24

18
+73

47
+35

49
+23

46
+36

36
+24

37
+44

Color:
60 and 70 = yellow
72 and 82 = brown
81 and 91 = green

Ohio is named for its state tree, the Ohio Buckeye. It has a hard seed like a chestnut.

C What is the state tree for your state?

38

Add two digits/regroup

Turkey Tracks

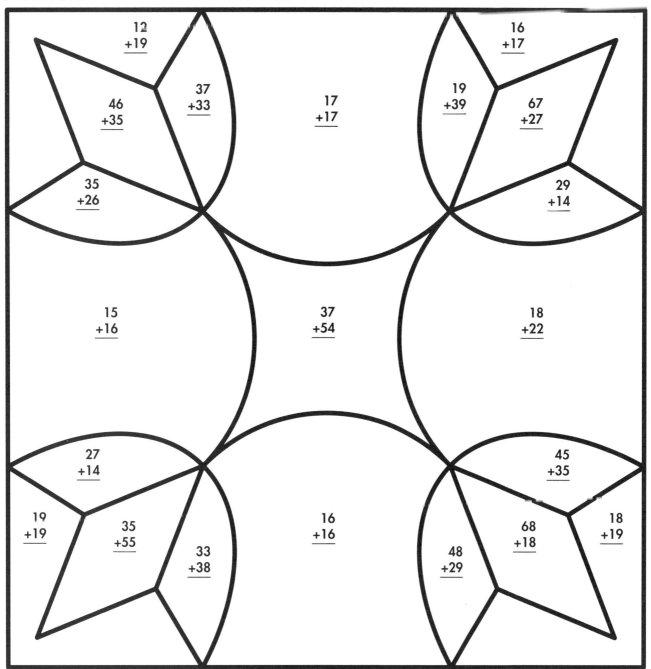

Color:

If the answer is from 1 to 40, color the space yellow.

If the answer is from 41 to 80, color the space orange.

If the answer is more than 80, color the space green.

Turkeys have webbed feet like ducks. This design was also called "Wandering Foot" because the footprints are heading away.

C On the back of this sheet of paper, write three things that people feel will bring bad luck.

39

Cross and Crown

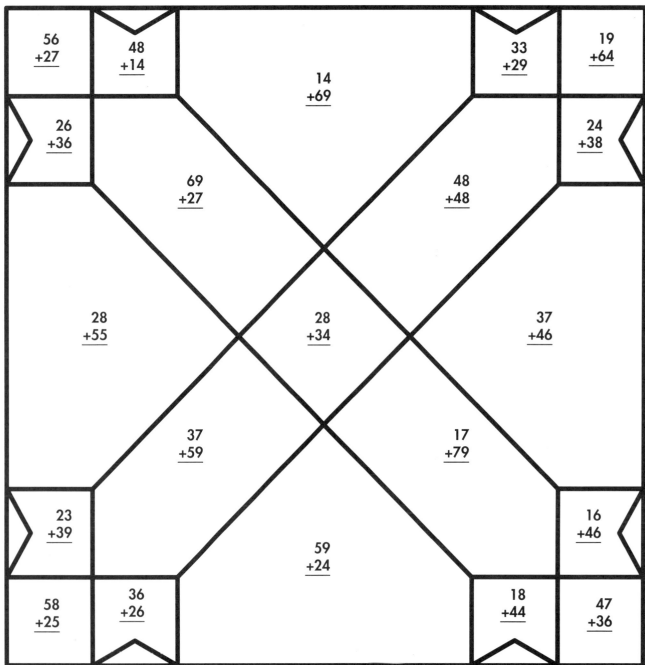

Color:

62 = red

83 = green

96 = blue

This picture honored the Church and the King of England.

C Make four addition problems using these numbers: 14, 16, 27, 38, 49, 56.

Sugar Loaf

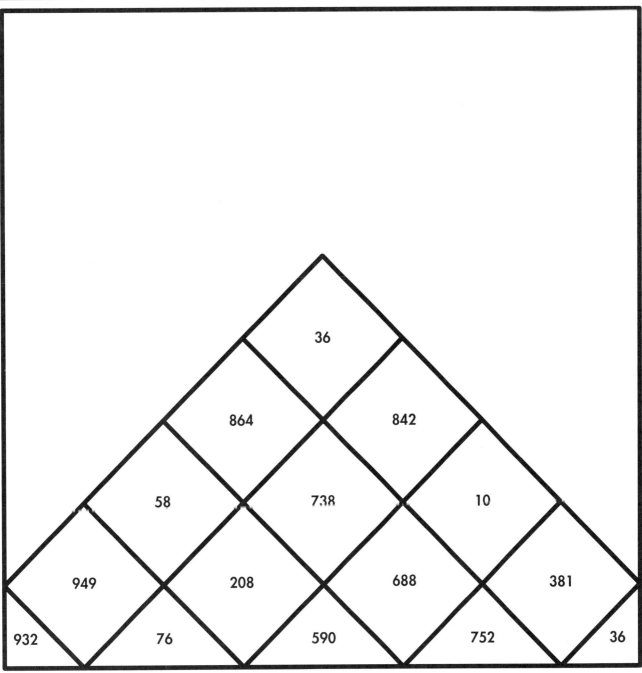

Color:

If the 1's place is odd, color the space red.

If the 10's place is odd, color the space blue.

If the 100's place is even, color the space orange.

In colonial days, sugar was molded into a cone shape and wrapped in blue paper before it was sold. Sugar cones were a rare treat because sugar was scarce.

C On the back of this sheet of paper, draw a picture of the sugar you have at home.

Square and Compass

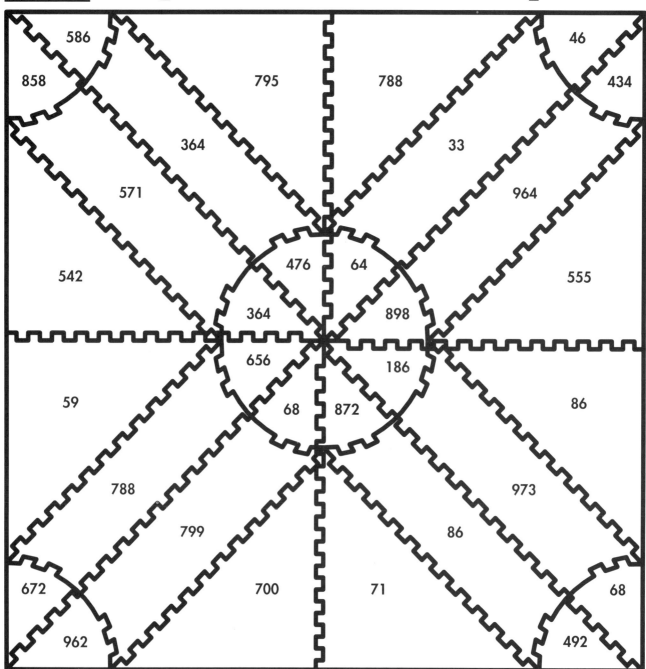

Color:

If the tens place is even, color it blue.

If the ones place is odd, color it green.

If the hundreds place is even, color it white.

The wife of a navy captain made up this quilt design.

C Using only numbers, write your birthday on the back of this sheet of paper. Underline all the even numbers, and circle the odd numbers.

The Little Giant

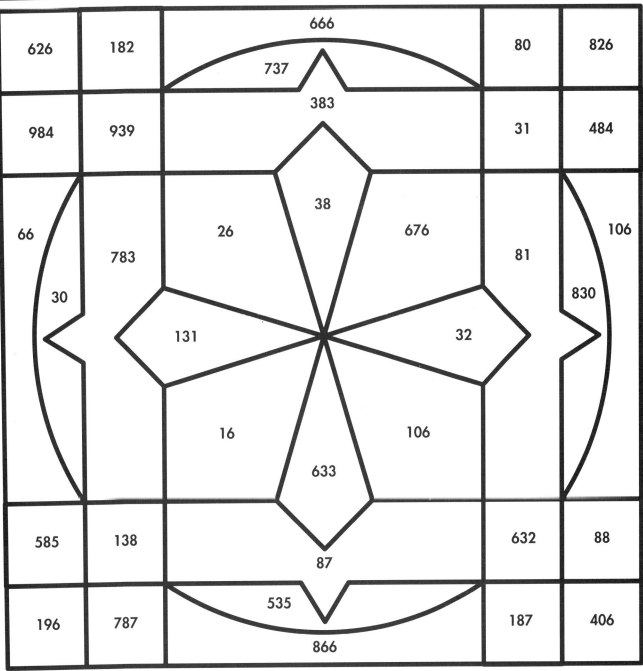

Color:

If the tens place is 3, color the space red.

If the ones place is 6, color the space green.

If the tens place is 8, color the space brown.

This picture was popular when Abraham Lincoln was elected President. But it was named for the loser in the election, Stephen Douglas.

C Lincoln was the sixteenth President. Write that number and circle the tens place on the back of this sheet of paper.

43

Storm at Sea

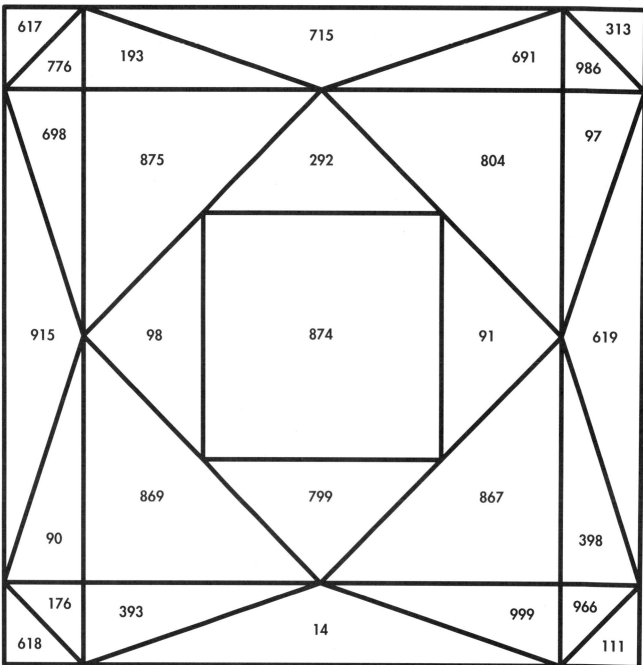

Color:

If the tens place is 1, color blue.

If the tens place is 9, color purple.

If the hundreds place is 8, color red.

If the hundreds place is 6, color black.

After you color this, tell why you think it was named "Storm at Sea."

C Write four numbers on the back of this sheet of paper. Make sure every tens place is odd.

44

Sunshine and Shadows

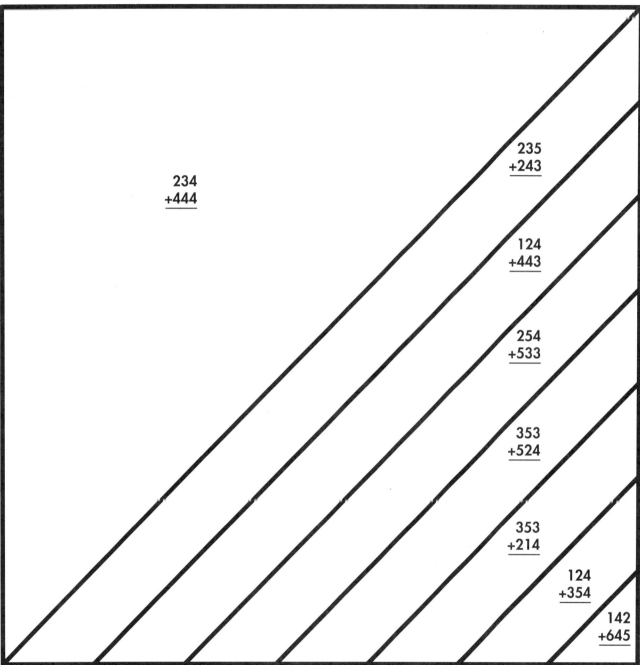

234
+444

235
+243

124
+443

254
+533

353
+524

353
+214

124
+354

142
+645

Color:

478 = yellow

567 = blue

678 = black

787 = red

877 = purple

This quilt may have been named by someone who was thinking of "happy times" (sunshine) and "sad times" (shadows).

C On the back of this sheet of paper, make two different problems that add up to 964.

Oak Leaf

Color:
  873 = red
  689 = brown
  425 = orange
  899 = yellow
  978 = green

Since the earliest colonial days, trees and leaves have been popular as quilt designs.

C Use three-digit numbers to make four math problems, each having the sum of 897.

46

Indian Hatchets

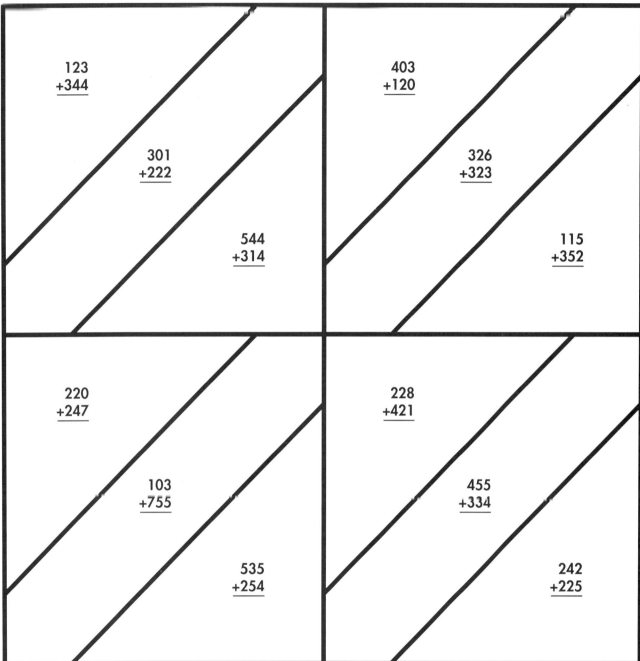

123
+344

301
+222

544
+314

403
+120

326
+323

115
+352

220
+247

103
+755

535
+254

228
+421

455
+334

242
+225

Color:

467 = yellow

523 = orange

649 = purple

789 = green

858 = red

This picture shows that pioneer men and women were afraid of Native Americans.

***C* On the back of this sheet of paper, make a three-digit addition problem using just odd numbers.**

Carnival Time

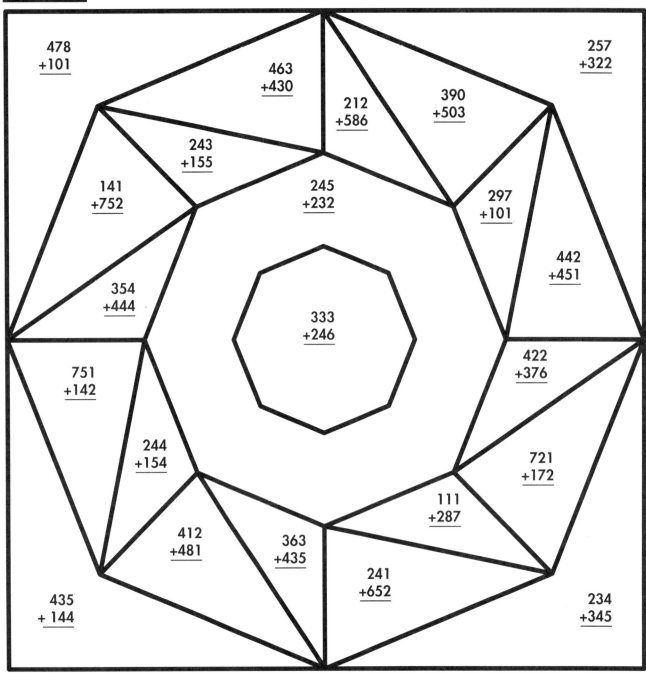

478
+101

463
+430

212
+586

390
+503

257
+322

243
+155

141
+752

245
+232

297
+101

354
+444

442
+451

333
+246

751
+142

422
+376

244
+154

721
+172

111
+287

412
+481

363
+435

241
+652

435
+ 144

234
+345

Color:
  398 = yellow
  477 = orange
  579 = purple
  798 = red
  893 = green

Take a good look at this pattern. Why do you think it was named "Carnival Time"?

_____

C On the back of this sheet of paper, draw a picture of your favorite carnival ride.

48

Cactus Flower

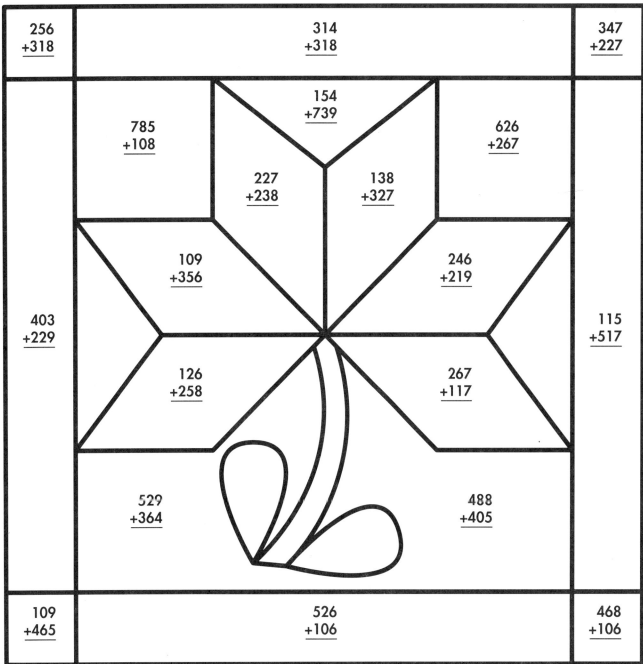

256
+318

314
+318

347
+227

154
+739

785
+108

626
+267

227
+238

138
+327

109
+356

246
+219

403
+229

115
+517

126
+258

267
+117

529
+364

488
+405

109
+465

526
+106

468
+106

Color:
384 = green
465 = orange
574 = brown
632 = red
893 = yellow

Even in the hot, dry desert a cactus
blooms with beautiful flowers.

C On the back of this sheet of paper,
use numbers to make fact families:
6, 7, 8, 9, 13, 14, 15, 16.

Nine-Patch Star

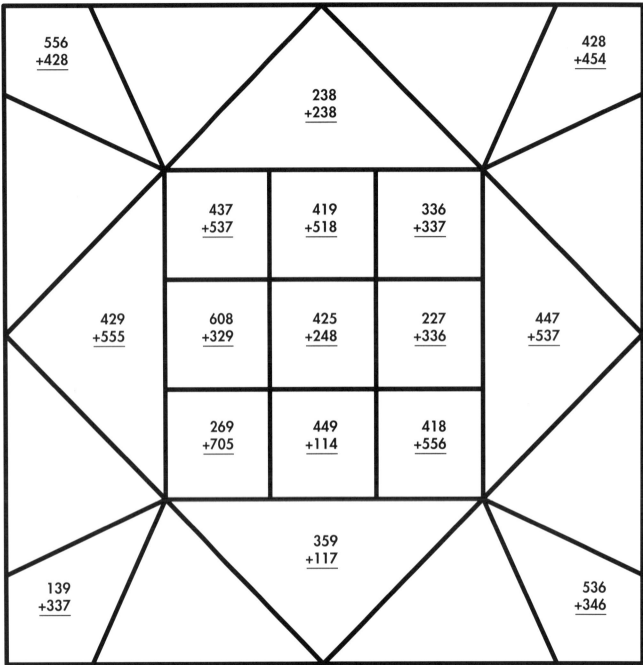

556
+428

428
+454

238
+238

437
+537

419
+518

336
+337

429
+555

608
+329

425
+248

227
+336

447
+537

269
+705

449
+114

418
+556

359
+117

139
+337

536
+346

Color:

563 and 937 = green
673 and 974 = red
476, 882, and 984 = black

Sometimes a name doesn't match a
pattern. This pattern has nine patches,
but where is the star?

C On the back of this sheet of paper,
draw a design that has four stars.
Give it a name.

Dutchman's Puzzle

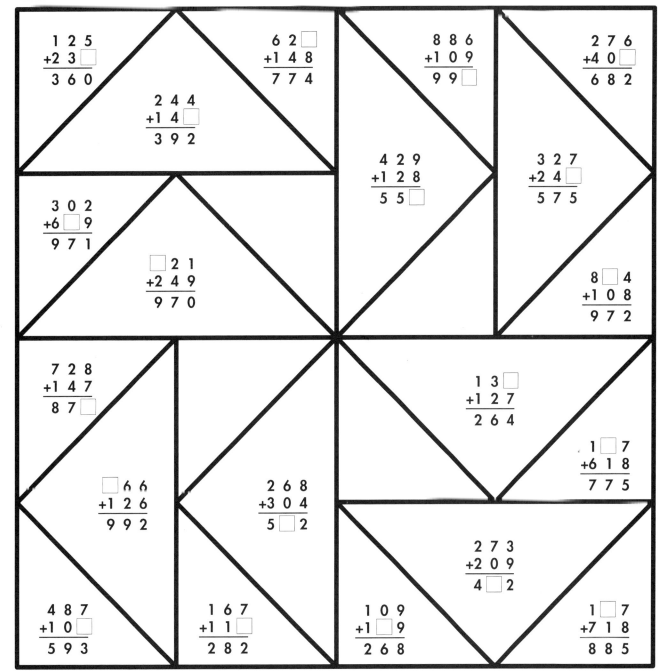

```
  1 2 5        6 2☐         8 8 6          2 7 6
+2 3☐        +1 4 8       +1 0 9         +4 0☐
  3 6 0        7 7 4         9 9☐           6 8 2

      2 4 4
    +1 4☐                    4 2 9          3 2 7
      3 9 2                +1 2 8        +2 4☐
                             5 5☐           5 7 5

  3 0 2
+6☐9
  9 7 1
        ☐2 1                               8☐4
      +2 4 9                             +1 0 8
        9 7 0                               9 7 2

  7 2 8
+1 4 7                            1 3☐
  8 7☐                          +1 2 7
                                  2 6 4

      ☐6 6                                   1☐7
    +1 2 6          2 6 8                  +6 1 8
      9 9 2        +3 0 4                    7 7 5
                    5☐2
                                    2 7 3
                                  +2 0 9
                                    4☐2

  4 8 7        1 6 7          1 0 9            1☐7
+1 0☐        +1 1☐          +1☐9          +7 1 8
  5 9 3        2 8 2          2 6 8            8 8 5
```

Color:
Fill in the blocks with
5, 6, 7, or 8, to complete
the problems.

5 and 6 = yellow

7 = blue

8 = red

If you traveled to Holland, you would see plenty of these in the countryside. What is in the design?_____

C On the back of this sheet of paper,
name something else for which HOLLAND
is famous.

51

 # Susannah!

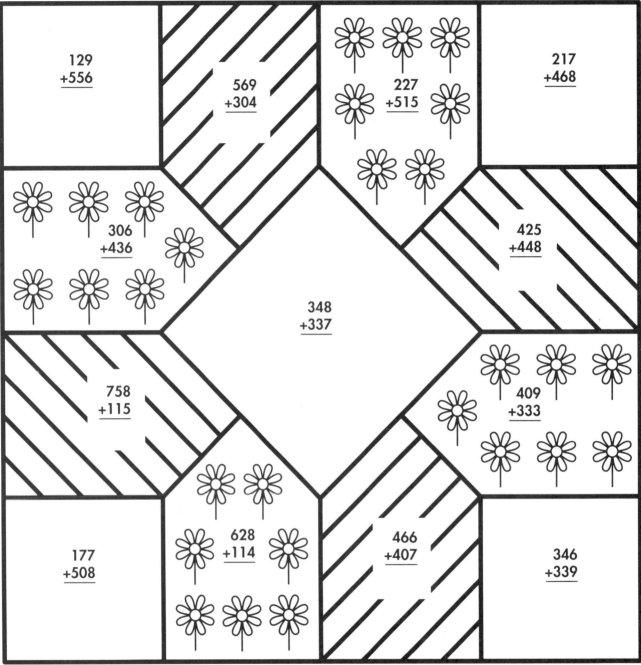

129
+556

569
+304

227
+515

217
+468

306
+436

425
+448

348
+337

758
+115

409
+333

177
+508

628
+114

466
+407

346
+339

Color:
685 = yellow
742 = blue
873 = green

While crossing the plains in wagon trains, pioneer women sang "Oh, Susannah!" and quilted the Susannah square. The points stand for mountain peaks ahead.

C Sing "Oh, Susannah!" with your class.

Tall Pine Tree

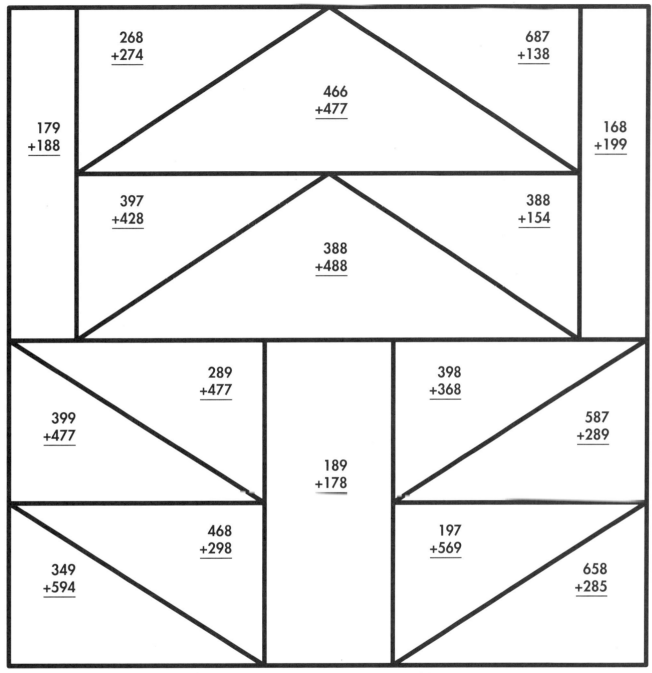

268
+274

687
+138

466
+477

179
+188

168
+199

397
+428

388
+154

388
+488

289
+477

398
+368

399
+477

587
+289

189
+178

468
+298

197
+569

349
+594

658
+285

Color:

367 = blue

766 = white

542 and 825 = yellow

876 and 943 = green

To the pioneers, the pine tree was a symbol for steadfastness and loyalty.

C Draw a pine tree on the back of this sheet of paper. Put five math facts, with regrouping, on it. Give it to a friend to do.

Chain of Diamonds

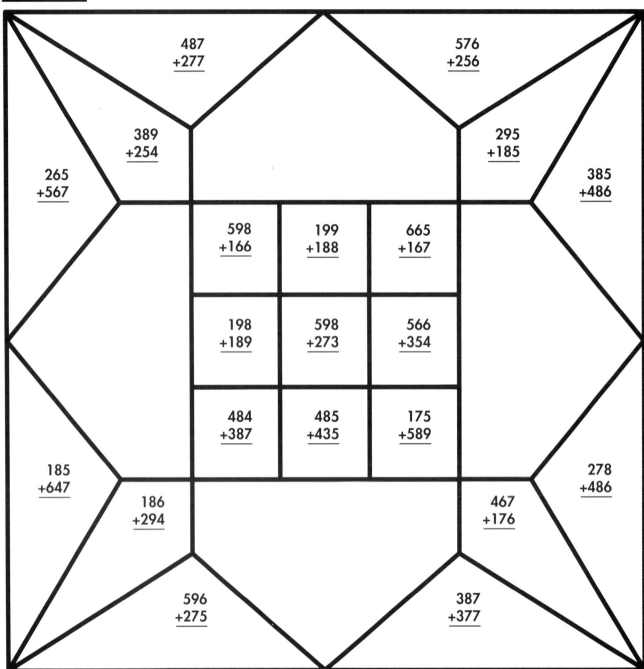

Color:

387 and 920 = orange
643 and 480 = blue
764, 832, and 871 = yellow

How many diamond shapes can you see in this design?

_____

C Look around the room and count the diamond shapes you can see. How many did you find?

Honey Bee

135
+269

776

748

157
+247

776

279
+265

569
+369

498
+278

776

589
+187

369
+258

378
+166

748

488
+139

387
+157

459
+479

748

238
+166

776

776

129
+275

Color:

404 = yellow
544 = blue
748 and 776 = green
627 = orange
938 = green

Can you see the honeybees buzzing in the corners of this picture?

C Herbert spent $3.88 on Monday and $2.39 on Tuesday. How much did he spend? Write the answer on the back of this sheet of paper.

Crosses and Losses

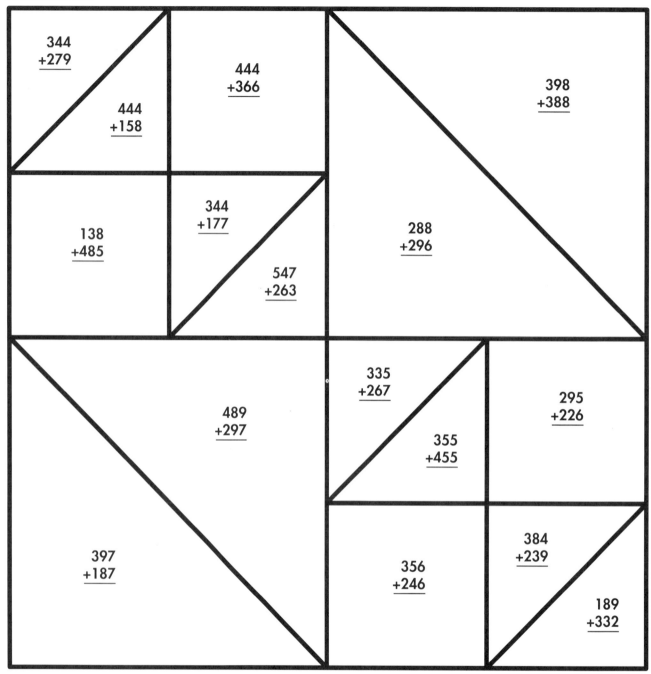

344
+279

444
+158

444
+366

398
+388

138
+485

344
+177

547
+263

288
+296

489
+297

335
+267

355
+455

295
+226

397
+187

356
+246

384
+239

189
+332

Color:

584 = purple

786 = red

521 and 602 = yellow

623 and 810 = green

It's hard to tell the meaning behind the name "Crosses and Losses." It's easier to tell why the name "Double X" is also used for this design.

C Write the best name for this picture on the back of this sheet of paper.

Memory Wreath

```
                22          54
                48          63
               +34         +54
          89                      38
          34                      34
         +14                     +21
 22          72          84
 47          57          88
+24         +57         +10


 47      66                 44      77
 33      65                 54      71
+24     +51                +88     +23
    88                         66
    24                         44
   +34                        +36

 87      86                 44      14
 42      68                 74      19
+42     +32                +64     +71


            95          63
            49          66
           +42         +53
       57                      44
       56                      24
 29   +24               55    +25
 14          28         53
+44         23         +63
           +53
```

Color:
 87 and 93 = red
 104 and 171 = yellow
 137 and 146 = blue
 182 and 186 = green

This design was usually made of pieces of cloth from the clothes of a loved one who had died.

C Turn to three pages in a book and write down the page numbers. Add the three pages numbers to find the sum. Work on the back of this sheet of paper.

Dove in the Window

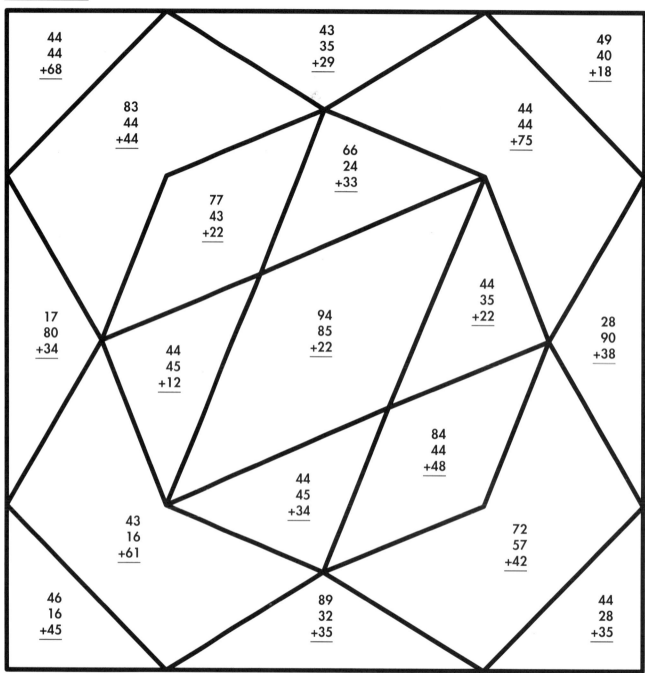

Color:
101 and 123 = orange
107 and 156 = yellow
171 and 163 = green
176 and 142 = brown
201 = red

In the early 1800s, the dove symbolized a happy marriage. Many girls made dove quilts before they got married.

C On the back of this sheet of paper, make a chart showing the number of times each answer appeared on this page.

Symbol

Quilt Name _____

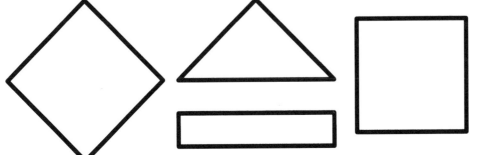

Cut out the shapes on left to use as patterns. Trace them in a design in this square. Color the design any way you want. Name your pattern, and draw a symbol for it.

**Quilt
Name** _____

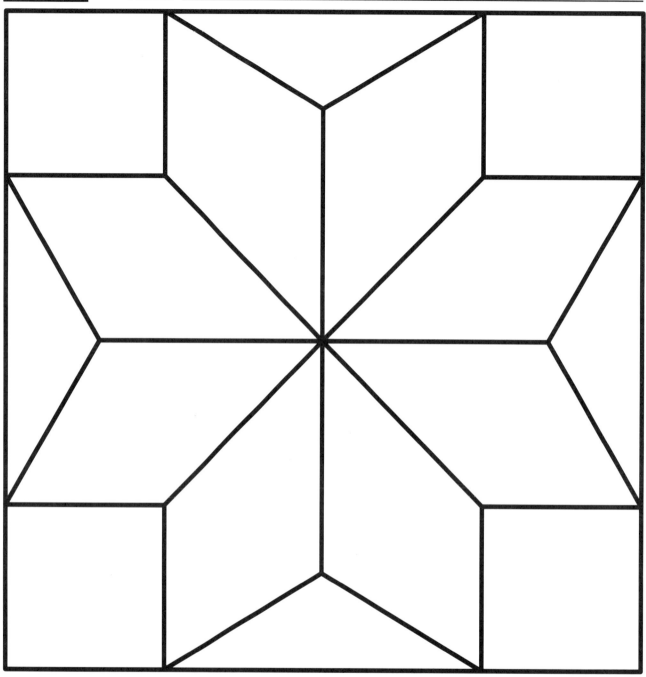

Look at this design. Use your imagination
to name this picture and tell why you chose
that name. Then color the picture.

Quilt Name _____

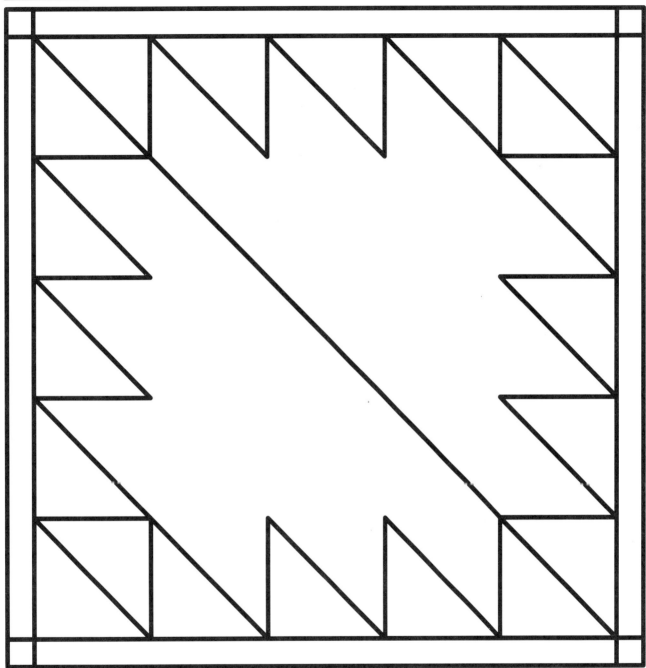

Color:

red = _____

blue = _____

green = _____

yellow = _____

Put an answer beside each color in the color code. (Your teacher may give you numbers to use.) Put math facts in each space to match the answers you are using.

 Heart Turnaround

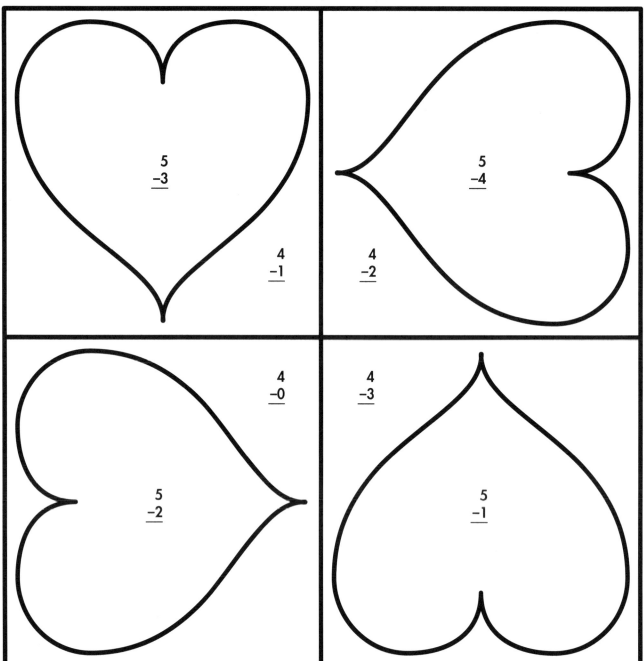

5
−3

4
−1

5
−4

4
−2

4
−0

4
−3

5
−2

5
−1

Color:
- 1 = red
- 2 = blue
- 3 = orange
- 4 = purple

It looks like the hearts are doing flips!

C Find the number 5 on the calendar. Write the name for the day on the back of this sheet of paper.

Hourglass

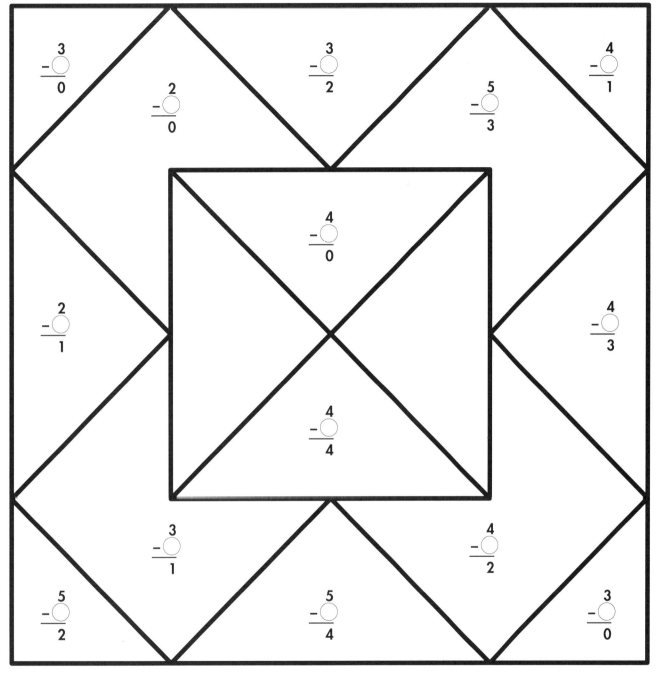

Color:

Put in the missing number to complete the problems.

0 and 4 = red

       1 = yellow

       2 = blue

       3 = green

Long ago, one way to tell the time was by using an hourglass. When all the sand dropped from the top to the bottom, one hour had gone by.

C Roll a dice two times. On the back of this sheet of paper, make a subtraction problem with the two numbers.

Tumbler

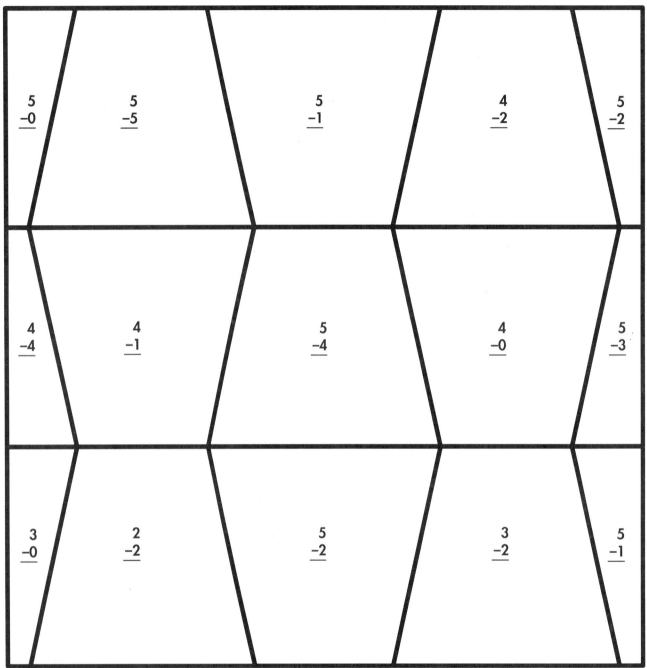

Color:

If the answer is
more than 2, color it blue.

If the answer is
less than 3, color it yellow.

A tumbler is a small drinking glass. How
many tumblers are in this picture?

_____

C Cut out the tumblers and use them for
   flashcards. (Cross out the answers first.)

 Garden

5 −3 5 −2 5 −1	5 −5	2 −0 3 −0 4 −0
5 −4	4 −0	3 −2
4 −1 5 −3 5 −0 3 −0 4 −2	3 −3	4 −1 4 −1 5 −1 5 −3 2 −0

Color:
0 and 1 = brown
2 and 3 = green
4 and 5 = red

Can you see the patches of flowers growing in the corners of the garden?

C Roll a dice two times. On the back of this sheet of paper, subtract the two numbers you roll.

Monkey Wrench

6 −4	9 −6	4 −2
8 −3	8 −4	10 −3
9 −1 10 −4	9 −0	8 −2 7 −4
8 −1	7 −3	8 −3
6 −3	10 −8	9 −1

Color:
2, 3, and 8 = green
4 and 6 = red
5 and 7 = brown
9 = black

Can you find the shape of a wrench in this picture?

C Cut numbers 7, 4, 5, 1, 2, 8, 3, 6, 10, and 9 out of a newspaper. Paste them, in order, on the back of this sheet of paper.

Ice Cream Bowl

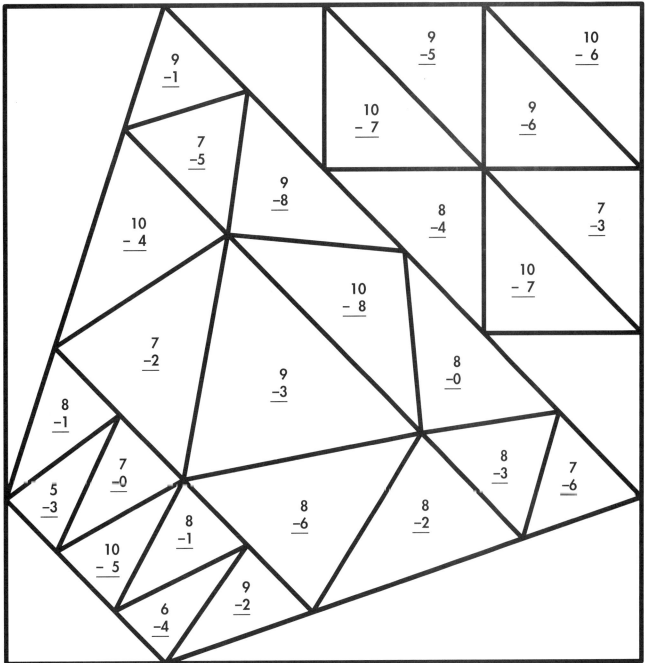

Color:

3 = red
6 = green
4 = orange
7 = purple
2 and 5 = yellow
1 and 8 = blue

Look for the big dish of ice cream in this picture.

C Find pages 4, 6, 8 in a book. On the back of this sheet of paper, write the first word that is on each page.

Road to Oklahoma

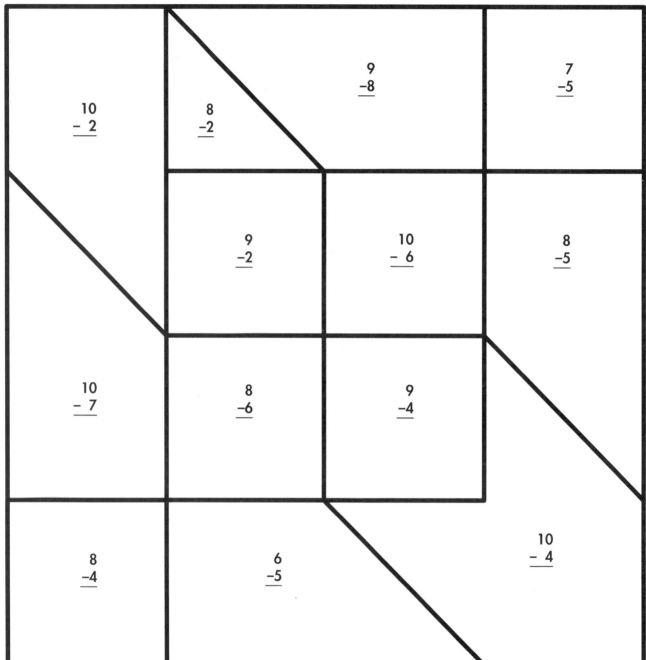

10 − 2	8 −2
	9 −8
	7 −5

9
−2

10
− 6

8
−5

10
− 7

8
−6

9
−4

8
−4

6
−5

10
− 4

Color:
1 and 3 = blue
2 and 4 = green
5 and 7 = brown
6 and 8 = yellow

As the pioneers settled different parts of the West, they named quilts to remember their journeys.

C On the back of this sheet of paper, write the names of three other states you know.

Pennsylvania Dutch

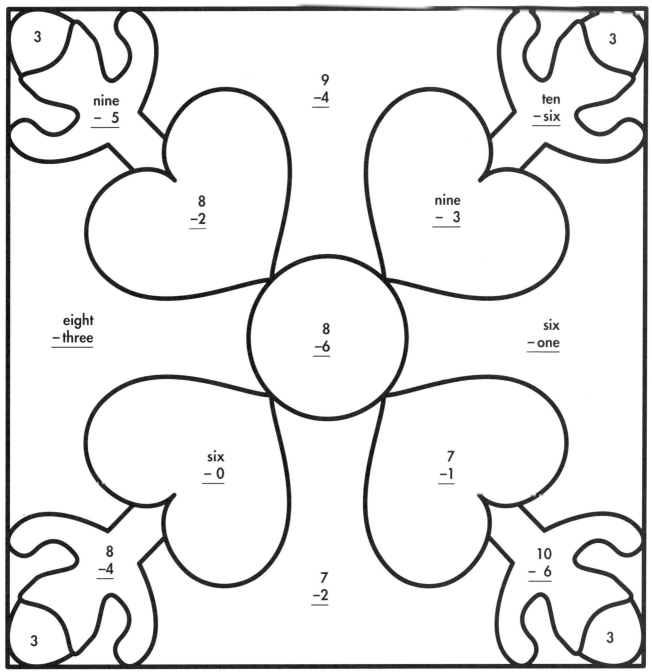

Color:
2 = yellow
3 = orange
4 = green
5 = blue
6 = red

This quilt is named for the Amish people, who settled in Pennsylvania. Amish people use hearts in many of their designs.

C Name your state and the state capitol on the back of this sheet of paper.

Indian Puzzle

11
− 8

11
− 9

14
− 8

14
− 6

14
− 9

13
− 6

11
− 4

11
− 7

14
− 8

14
− 7

13
− 5

12
− 3

12
− 9

12
− 3

11
− 8

11
− 7

14
− 6

13
− 9

14
− 6

11
− 9

11
− 9

12
− 4

12
− 8

11
− 3

11
− 9

12
− 9

14
− 5

11
− 8

12
− 6

12
− 5

11
− 2

11
− 8

11
− 3

13
− 8

13
− 7

11
− 5

13
− 9

11
− 3

12
− 9

12
− 7

Color:
2, 3, and 4 = brown
5, 6, and 7 = red
8 and 9 = yellow

These colors were often worn by Native Americans. They used roots and berries to make dye to color cloth.

C On the back of this sheet of paper, write three subtraction families for 11 and 12.

70

Liberty Star

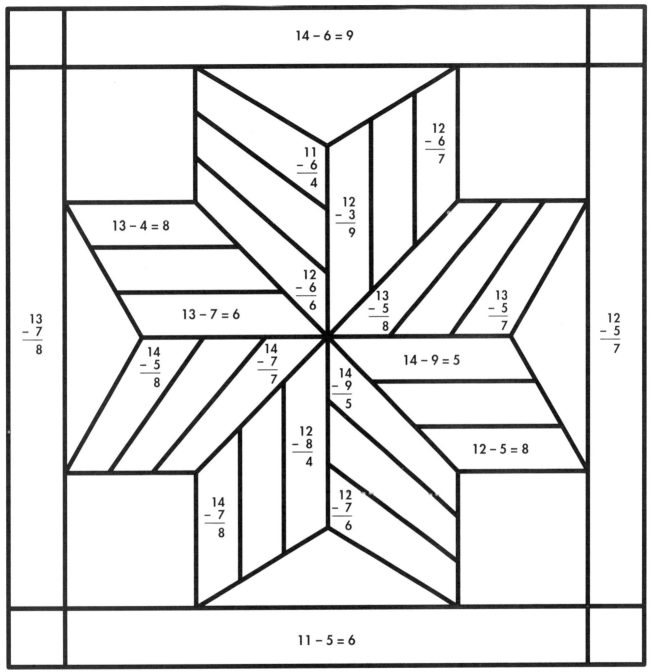

The figure contains the following subtraction problems:

$14 - 6 = 9$

$11 - 6 = 4$ (written as $\frac{-6}{4}$ under 11)

$12 - 6 = 7$

$12 - 3 = 9$

$13 - 4 = 8$

$12 - 6 = 6$

$13 - 7 = 6$

$13 - 5 = 8$

$13 - 5 = 7$

$13 - 7 = 8$

$12 - 5 = 7$

$14 - 5 = 8$

$14 - 7 = 7$

$14 - 9 = 5$

$14 - 9 = 5$

$12 - 8 = 4$

$12 - 5 = 8$

$14 - 7 = 8$

$12 - 7 = 6$

$11 - 5 = 6$

Color:

If the answer is correct, color the space red.

If the answer is wrong, color the space blue.

Red, white, and blue are the colors of the American flag. They have come to mean liberty to people all over the world.

C Find another symbol of liberty in a magazine or newspaper.

Mill Wheel

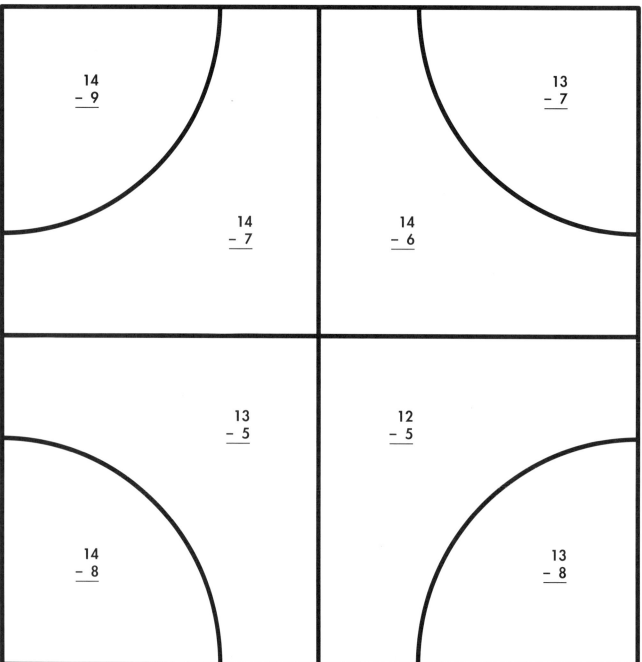

Color:
5 and 6 = red
7 and 8 = blue

This design honors the mill that ground wheat into flour. Of course, that was in Great-Grandpa's day.

C Say the facts for 13 and 14 out loud to a friend.

Stonemason's Puzzle

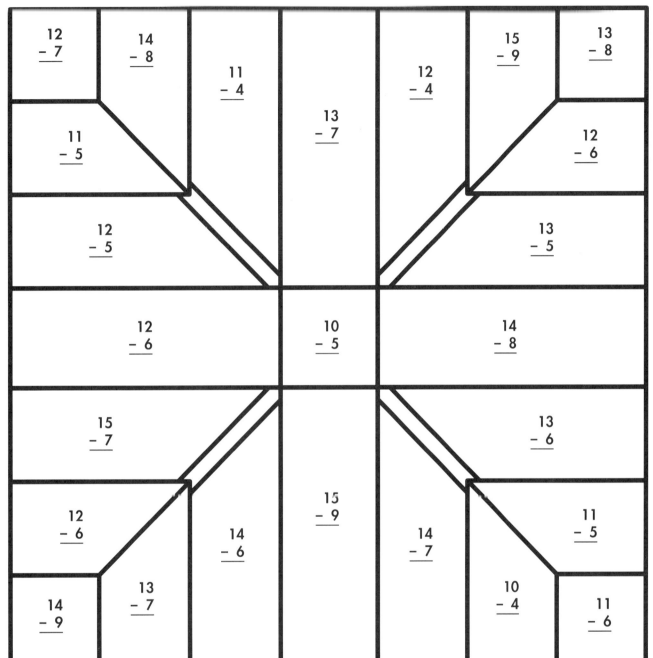

Color:

5 = green

6 = yellow

7 = orange

8 = blue

This picture honored the builders of the day, especially the men who laid the stone to build the strong buildings.

C On the back of this sheet of paper, list the names of four trades of today.

Crossroads to Texas

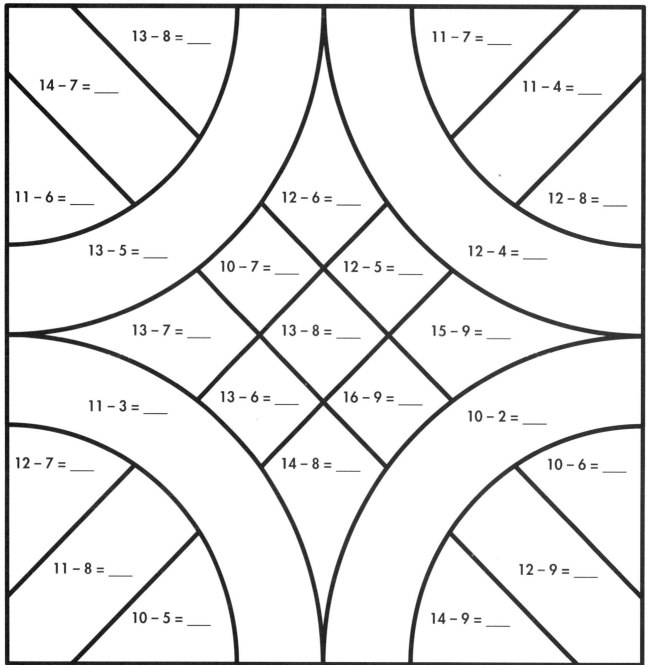

13 − 8 = ___

14 − 7 = ___

11 − 7 = ___

11 − 4 = ___

11 − 6 = ___

12 − 6 = ___

12 − 8 = ___

13 − 5 = ___

12 − 4 = ___

10 − 7 = ___   12 − 5 = ___

13 − 7 = ___   13 − 8 = ___   15 − 9 = ___

13 − 6 = ___   16 − 9 = ___

11 − 3 = ___   10 − 2 = ___

12 − 7 = ___   14 − 8 = ___   10 − 6 = ___

11 − 8 = ___   12 − 9 = ___

10 − 5 = ___   14 − 9 = ___

Color:
4 and 5 = red
3 and 7 = green
      6 = yellow
      8 = brown

While traveling west to Texas, the pioneers may have had a few problems deciding which road to take!

C **Pretend you are traveling west to Texas. On the back of this sheet of paper, name four states you would have to travel through to get there.**

74

Prairie Flower

$14 - 5 =$ ___

$18 - 9 =$ ___

$\begin{array}{r} 11 \\ -\ 8 \\ \hline \end{array}$ $\begin{array}{r} 16 \\ -\ 7 \\ \hline \end{array}$ $\begin{array}{r} 12 \\ -\ 9 \\ \hline \end{array}$

$14 - 9 =$ ___

$14 - 8 =$ ___

$12 - 4 =$ ___

$12 - 8 =$ ___

$\begin{array}{r} 13 \\ -\ 8 \\ \hline \end{array}$

$\begin{array}{r} 14 \\ -\ 9 \\ \hline \end{array}$

$\begin{array}{r} 12 \\ -\ 6 \\ \hline \end{array}$

$\begin{array}{r} 13 \\ -\ 7 \\ \hline \end{array}$

$\begin{array}{r} 12 \\ -\ 7 \\ \hline \end{array}$

$\begin{array}{r} 15 \\ -\ 8 \\ \hline \end{array}$

$\begin{array}{r} 12 \\ -\ 5 \\ \hline \end{array}$

$\begin{array}{r} 13 \\ -\ 6 \\ \hline \end{array}$

$\begin{array}{r} 11 \\ -\ 5 \\ \hline \end{array}$

$\begin{array}{r} 15 \\ -\ 9 \\ \hline \end{array}$

$\begin{array}{r} 14 \\ -\ 9 \\ \hline \end{array}$

$\begin{array}{r} 16 \\ -\ 9 \\ \hline \end{array}$

$\begin{array}{r} 11 \\ -\ 5 \\ \hline \end{array}$

Color:

3 = orange
4 = yellow
5, 6, and 7 = green
8 = blue
9 = red

The pioneers saw many beautiful wild flowers in bloom as they crossed the prairie.

C On the back of this sheet of paper, write the number words in order from 11 to 18.

Rocky Road to Kansas

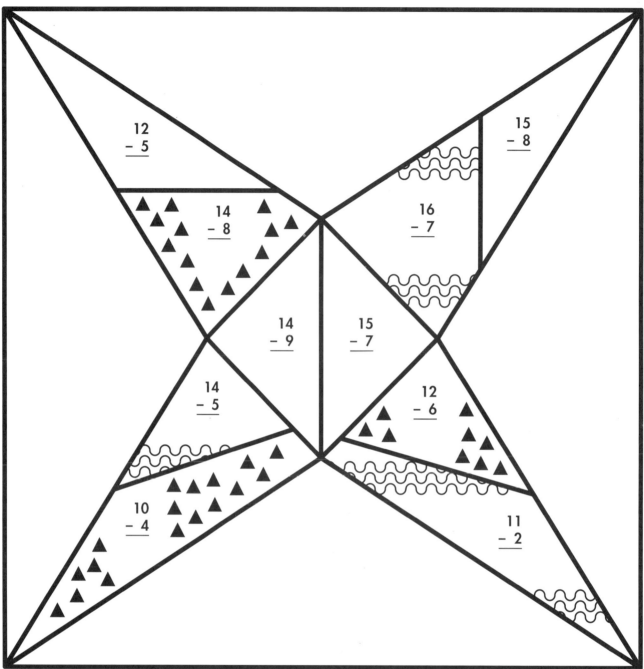

Color:
- 5 = yellow
- 6 = brown
- 7 = green
- 8 = orange
- 9 = blue

Crossing the country in a covered wagon was a hard trip. Rivers and rocks were some of the dangers. Can you find the shapes?

C On the back of this sheet of paper, write a story about the pioneers' trip west.

Bridal Wreath

Color:

    5 = brown

    6 = green

7 and 8 = red

This picture was usually put into a quilt for a couple who were going to be married. Relatives of the bride would make it and the bride was not allowed to help in any way.

C On the back of this sheet of paper, write all the facts you can using these numbers: 6, 7, 14, 13, 8, 9, 15.

World's Fair

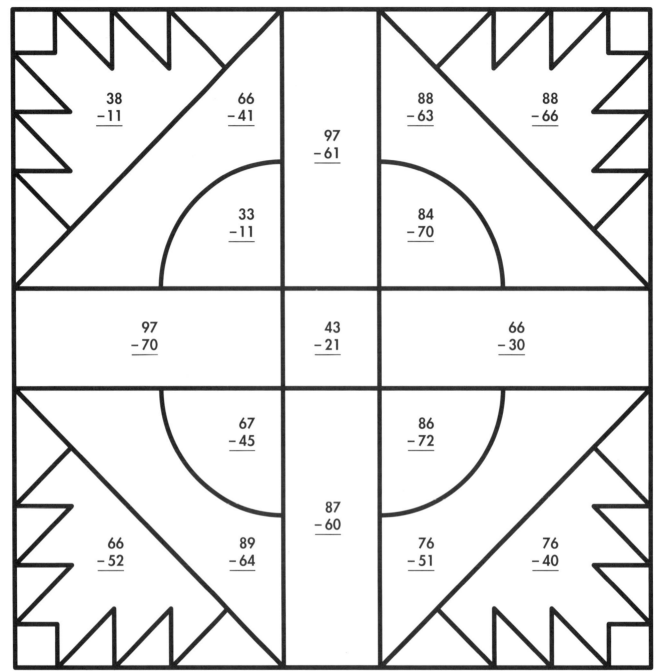

Color:
14 and 22 = red
25 = green
27 and 36 = blue

This quilt won a First Prize blue ribbon at the Chicago World's Fair in 1893.

C On the back of this sheet of paper, write the number that comes before and after 87, 66, and 98.

Fool's Puzzle

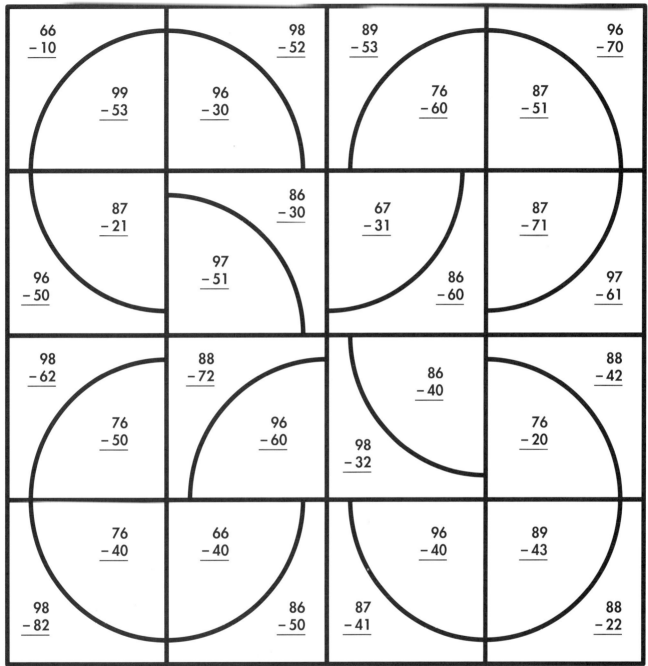

66
− 10

99
− 53

98
− 52

96
− 30

89
− 53

76
− 60

96
− 70

87
− 51

87
− 21

96
− 50

86
− 30

97
− 51

67
− 31

86
− 60

87
− 71

97
− 61

98
− 62

76
− 50

88
− 72

96
− 60

98
− 32

86
− 40

88
− 42

76
− 20

76
− 40

98
− 82

66
− 40

86
− 50

87
− 41

96
− 40

89
− 43

88
− 22

Color:

16 = green
26 = yellow
36 = orange
46 = red
56 = blue
66 = brown

When you are finished with this page, cut the four inside squares apart and put the puzzle together correctly.

C On the back of this sheet of paper, write two numbers larger than 85 and two numbers smaller than 94.

79

Pullman Puzzle

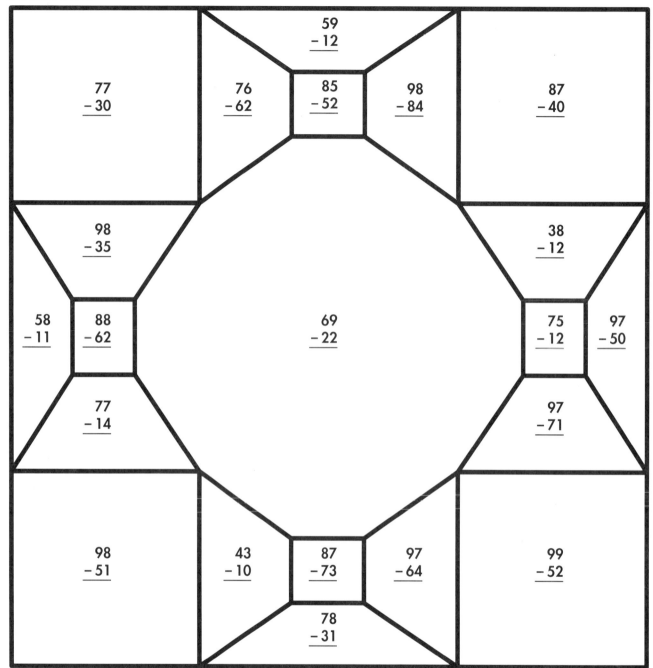

Color:
- 14 = red
- 26 = purple
- 33 = blue
- 47 = yellow
- 63 = green

When you are finished with this picture, you will know what the porters on trains used to wear under their chins.

C On the back of this paper, write five words to describe trains you have seen.

Jack in the Box

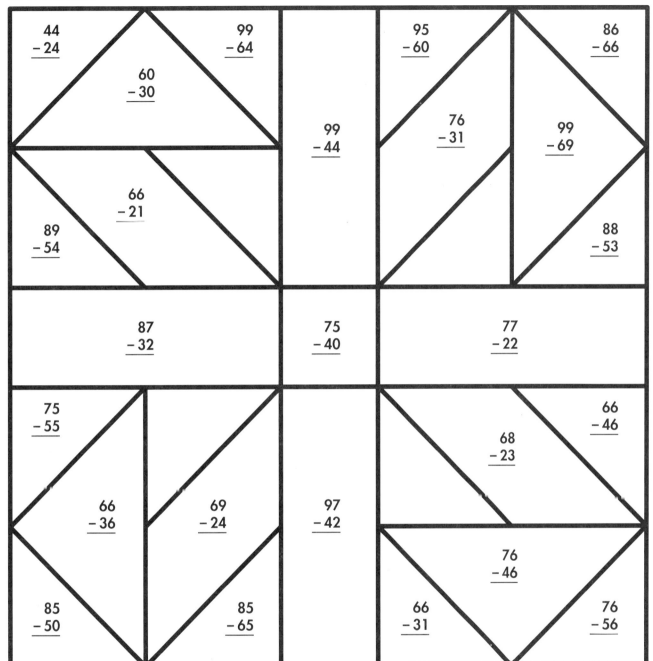

Color:

20 and 35 = green

30 = red

45 = purple

55 = black

This picture does not resemble the name at all! Why do you think it has the name "Jack in the Box"?

_____

C On the back of this sheet of paper, make a two-digit subtraction problem using only number words.

Forever Friends

| 92
− 48 | 95
− 59 | 83
− 25 | 94
− 58 | 81
− 37 |

73
− 37

90
− 46

82
− 46

94
− 36

91
− 33

92
− 34

74
− 38

92
− 56

71
− 35

| 60
− 16 | 80
− 44 | 70
− 12 | 90
− 54 | 73
− 29 |

Color:

36 = yellow
44 = blue
58 = red

This picture represents a long friendship between two people.

C Write the names of five of your friends on the back of this sheet of paper.

82

Butterflies

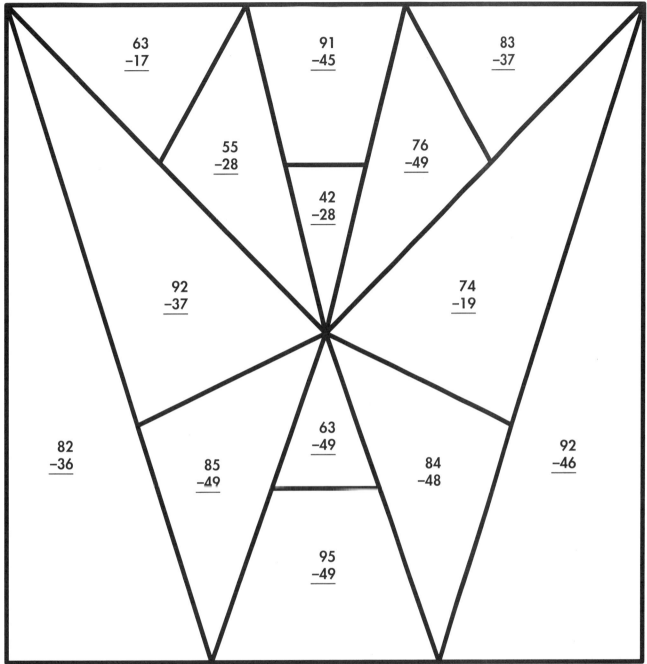

63
−17

91
−45

83
−37

55
−28

76
−49

42
−28

92
−37

74
−19

82
−36

85
−49

63
−49

84
−48

92
−46

95
−49

Color:
14 = brown
27 = red
36 = orange
46 = blue
55 = yellow

Many colored butterflies in a summer garden were probably the inspiration for this design.

C Do this problem on the back of this sheet of paper: Eight tens and three ones *minus* four tens and seven ones.

Indian Trails

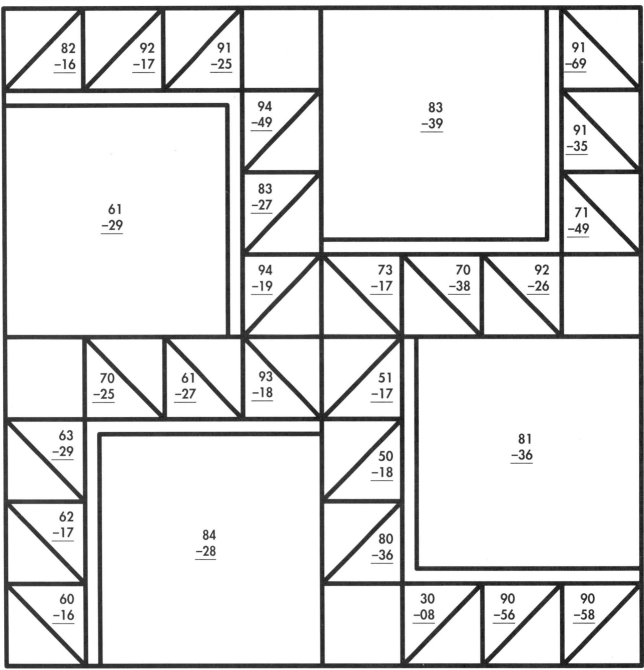

Color:
22 and 32 = blue
56 and 66 = orange
34 and 44 = red
45 and 75 = brown

Some Native Americans found that the best way to stay safe in the woods was to make a zig-zag trail.

C On the back of this sheet of paper, write 5 two-digit numbers. Circle the tens place and underline the ones place in each number.

Maple Leaf

```
 83      85
-19     -59
```

```
 72      81      81
-18     -38     -27
```

```
 63                      75
-37                     -49

 92      81      61
-49     -17     -18

 93                      91
-29                     -27
```

```
         62      92
        -19     -38
```

```
 73      72      44
-19     -08     -18
```

Color:

43 = orange
54 = green
26 and 64 = brown

This design honors the maple tree because of the delicious syrup people make from its sap.

C Cut and paste numbers from the newspaper on the back of this sheet of paper. Make a two-digit subtraction problem that uses regrouping.

Barbara Frietchie's Star

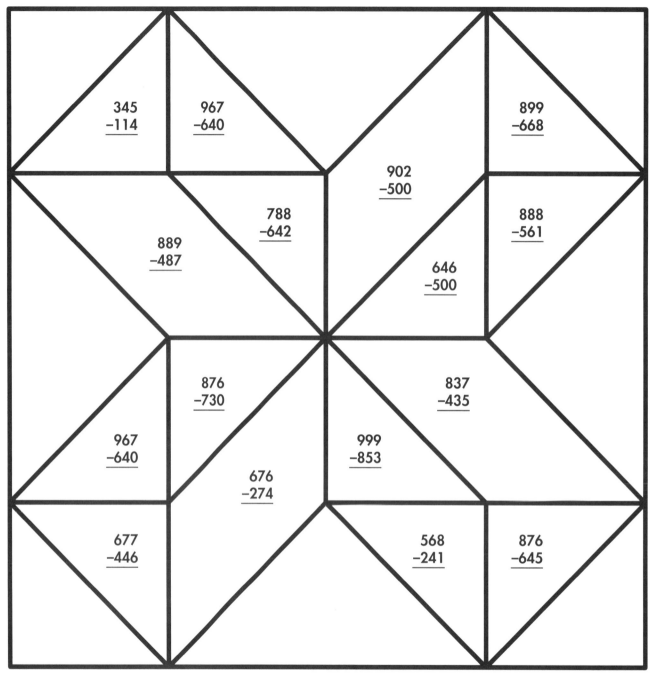

345
−114

967
−640

899
−668

902
−500

788
−642

889
−487

888
−561

646
−500

876
−730

837
−435

967
−640

999
−853

676
−274

677
−446

568
−241

876
−645

Color:

146 = yellow
231 = red
327 = green
402 = blue

Barbara Frietchie, born in 1766, was the subject of the poem by John Greenleaf Whittier. She was a heroine for the ladies of the time, and so a quilt was named in her honor.

C Write two problems from this page on the back of this sheet of paper. Use decimal points and dollar signs to represent money.

Birds in the Air

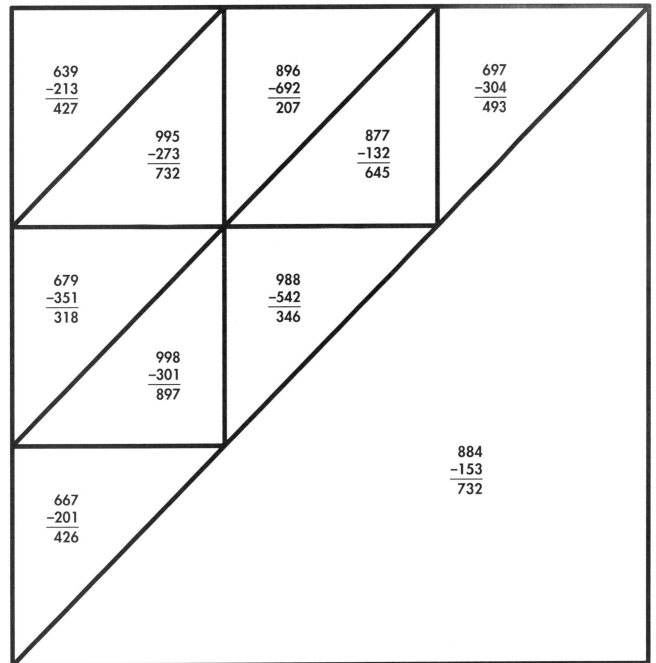

In each answer, one number is incorrect. Cross out the wrong number and write the correct number below it.

If the correct answer is from 200 to 500, color the space blue.

If the correct answer is from 600 to 900, color the space white.

Look for the birds flying into the blue sky.

C On the back of this sheet of paper, write the names of three birds you have seen.

87

Rambler

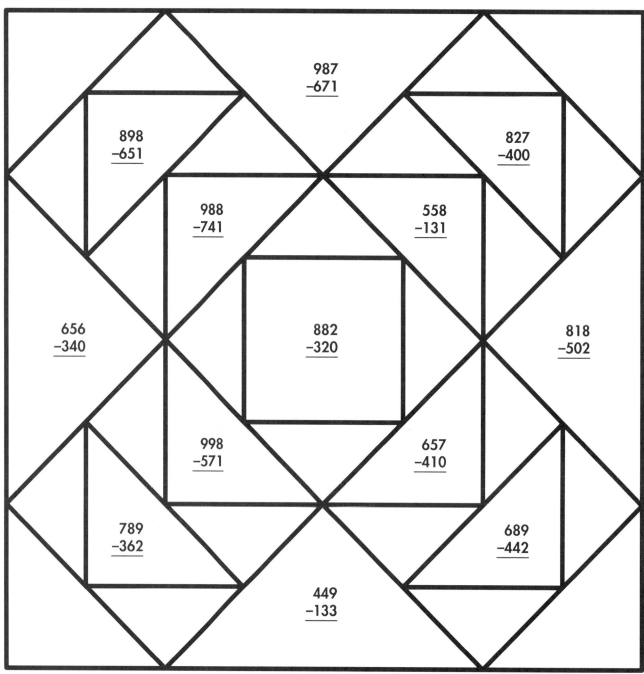

987
−671

898
−651

827
−400

988
−741

558
−131

656
−340

882
−320

818
−502

998
−571

657
−410

789
−362

689
−442

449
−133

Color:

247 = purple
316 = green
427 = red
562 = blue

This picture shows the path a rambler's wanderings may take him or her. A rambler can go in any direction.

C On the back of this sheet of paper, write the numbers from 320 to 368. You must count by twos.

88

Checkerboard Heart

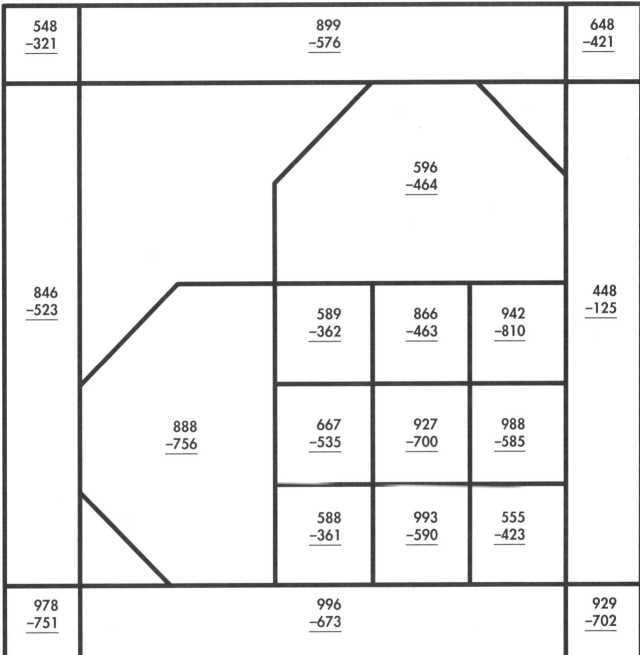

548
−321

899
−576

648
−421

846
−523

596
−464

448
−125

589
−362

866
−463

942
−810

888
−756

667
−535

927
−700

988
−585

588
−361

993
−590

555
−423

978
−751

996
−673

929
−702

Create a color code for the answers given below:

132 = _____

227 = _____

323 = _____

403 = _____

This is one way to make a pretty heart decoration.

C Draw three hearts on the back of this sheet of paper. On each heart, make a problem that has 273 as the answer.

89

Martha Washington's Star

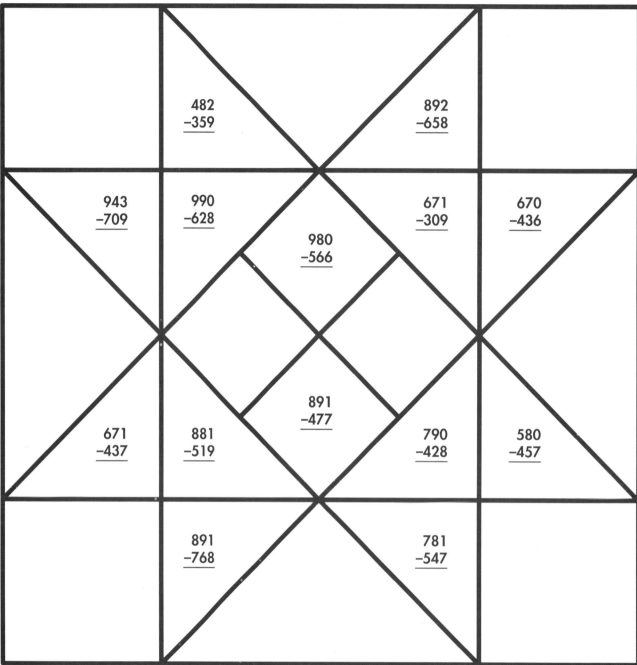

482
−359

892
−658

943
−709

990
−628

671
−309

670
−436

980
−566

891
−477

671
−437

881
−519

790
−428

580
−457

891
−768

781
−547

Color:
123 and 234 = red
362 = green
414 = blue

The women of George Washington's time loved and respected the first President's wife, Martha. They honored her with this design.

C On the back of this sheet of paper, write three Presidents' names. Then look up the names of their wives.

Nelson's Victory

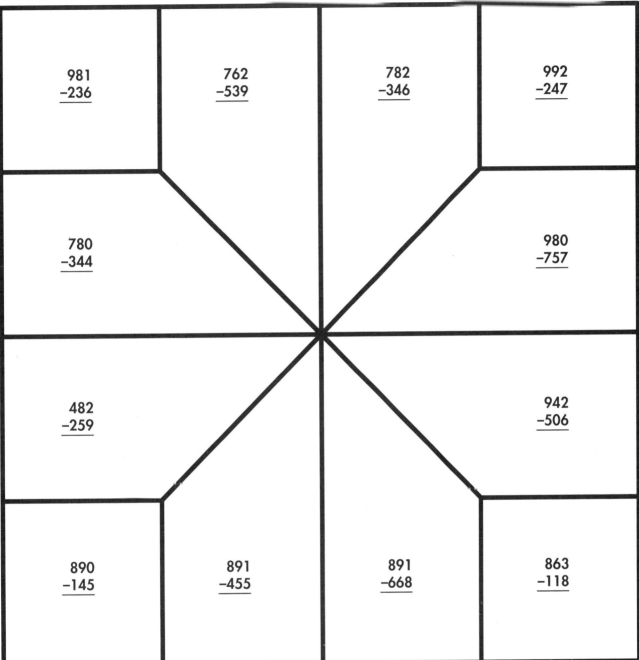

```
  981        762        782        992
 -236       -539       -346       -247

  780                             980
 -344                            -757

  482                             942
 -259                            -506

  890        891        891        863
 -145       -455       -668       -118
```

Color:

223 = red
436 = orange
745 = black

This design honors naval hero Viscount Nelson, who won the battle against Napoleon's forces. The victory ended the French hope of invading England.

C On the back of this sheet of paper, subtract your age from 762. When you have the answer, subtract your age again. Do this three more times.

Fly Foot

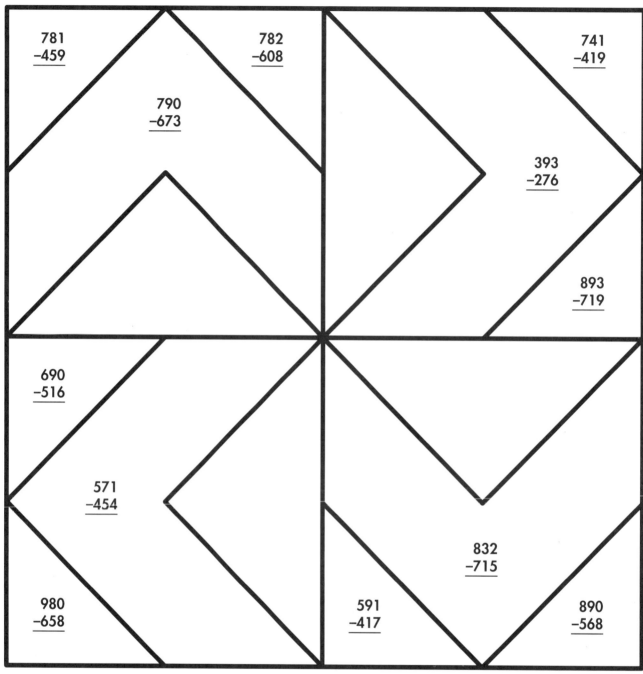

781
−459

782
−608

741
−419

790
−673

393
−276

893
−719

690
−516

571
−454

832
−715

980
−658

591
−417

890
−568

Color:
117 = blue
174 = green
322 = red

This design looks like the footprint of a fly. It also looks like eight thin fly's legs.

***

C Choose a problem on this page. Write it on the back of this sheet of paper using words instead of numbers.

92

Cornucopia

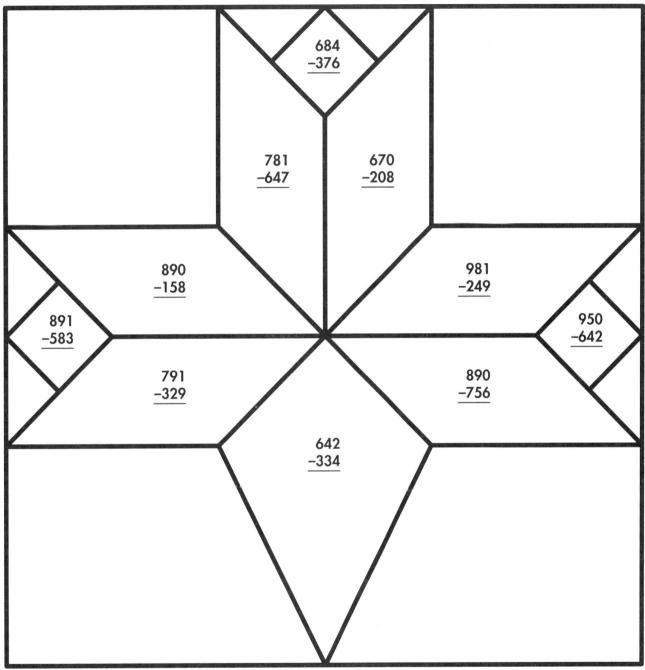

Color:
- 134 = orange
- 308 = green
- 462 = red
- 732 = purple

The cornucopia is a hollow, horn-shaped dish. At harvest time and Thanksgiving people put vegetables in this kind of dish.

C On the back of this sheet of paper, write three things you are thankful for at Thanksgiving.

Wind Blown Square

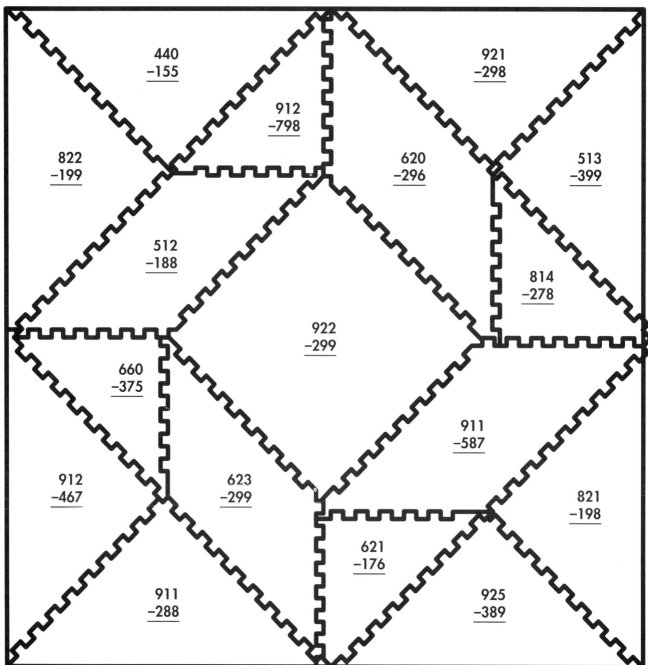

440
−155

912
−798

921
−298

822
−199

620
−296

513
−399

512
−188

814
−278

922
−299

660
−375

911
−587

912
−467

623
−299

821
−198

911
−288

621
−176

925
−389

Color:
114 = orange
285 = blue
324 = green
445 = purple
536 = brown
623 = black

This design may have been drawn by someone who lived in a very windy area.

C Write five numbers from this page on the back of this sheet of paper. Round them to the nearest hundred.

Kansas Dugout

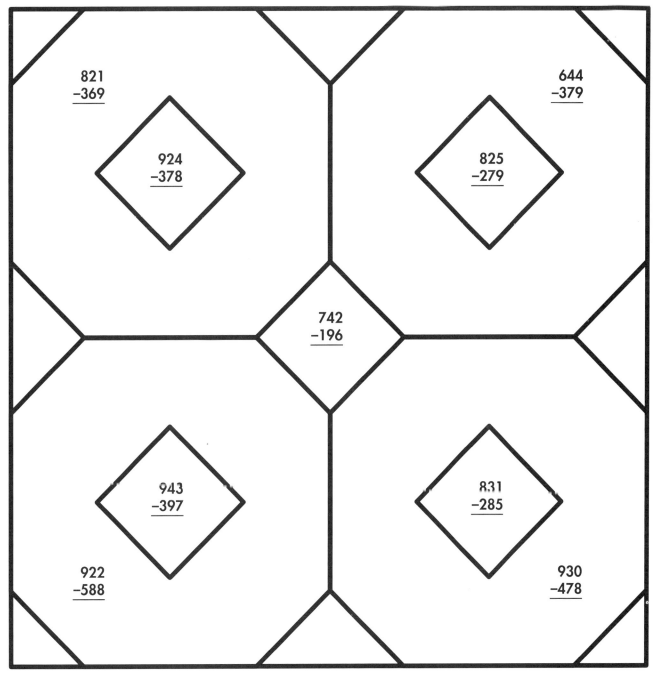

821
−369

644
−379

924
−378

825
−279

742
−196

943
−397

831
−285

922
−588

930
−478

Color:
265 = red
334 = green
452 = yellow
546 = black

On the trip west, some pioneers slept in tents or wagons. Others dug holes in the ground to shelter themselves from the winds.

C On the back of this sheet of paper, write a story problem using one problem from this page.

Little Red Schoolhouse

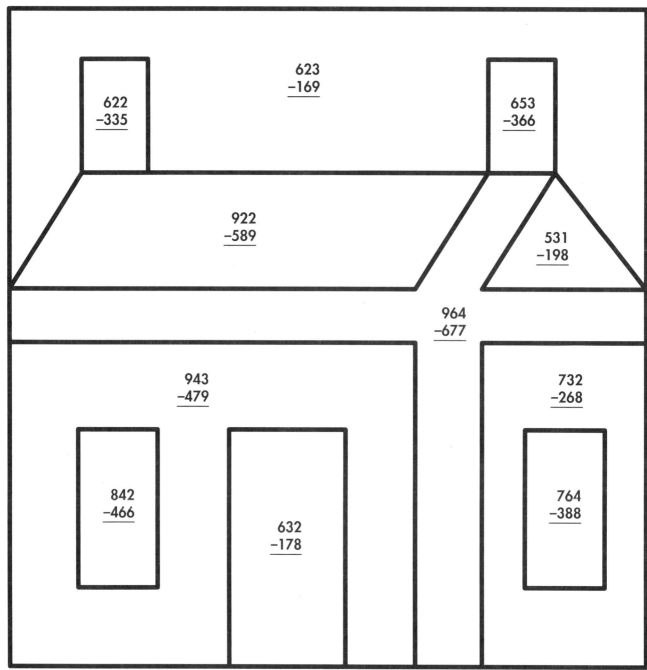

Color:
  287 = black
  333 = brown
  376 = yellow
  454 = blue
  464 = red

Long ago, schools were usually small buildings with a single room. One teacher had students from the first grade through the eighth grade.

C Look in tonight's newspaper for a sentence that uses a number word. Write the sentence on the back of this sheet of paper.

Philadelphia Pavements

636
−198

923
−597

627
−189

954
−378

973
−299

644
−399

762
−186

826
−388

624
−298

731
−486

622
−184

544
−299

825
−499

962
−288

951
−277

741
−496

831
−255

923
−347

862
−188

625
−299

933
−259

Color:

245 and 576 = black

438 and 674 = green

326 = red

This picture honors the "City of Brotherly Love"—Philadelphia, Pennsylvania.

C Draw a map of your neighborhood on the back of this sheet of paper. Write directions that tell how to go to a friend's house from yours.

King's Crown

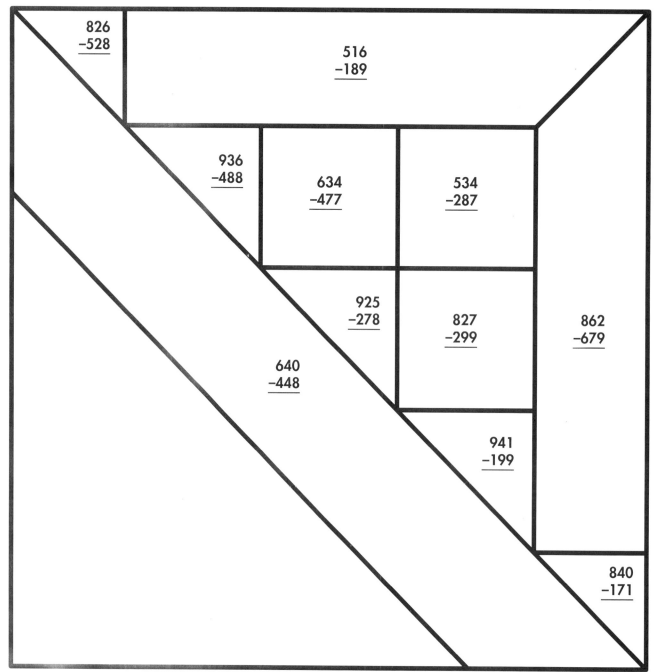

826
−528

516
−189

936
−488

634
−477

534
−287

925
−278

827
−299

862
−679

640
−448

941
−199

840
−171

If the answer has:
3—color blue
4—color red
5—color white
9—color yellow

This design was named to honor Napoleon. In many pictures, he wears a pointed hat.

C On the back of this sheet of paper, write the names of two countries and the leaders of those countries.

Jackson's Star

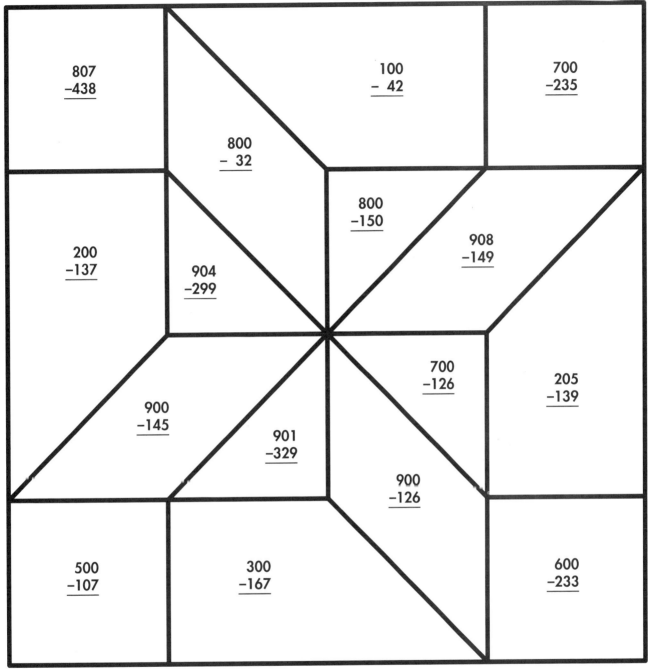

807
−438

100
− 42

700
−235

800
− 32

800
−150

908
−149

200
−137

904
−299

900
−145

700
−126

205
−139

901
−329

900
−126

500
−107

300
−167

600
−233

If the answer is from:
   50 to 250—color yellow
300 to 500—color blue
550 to 700—color white
750 to 900—color red

This star picture was created to honor Andrew Jackson, the seventh President of the United States.

C Counting by twos, write the numbers from 600 to 620 on the back of this sheet of paper.

White House Steps

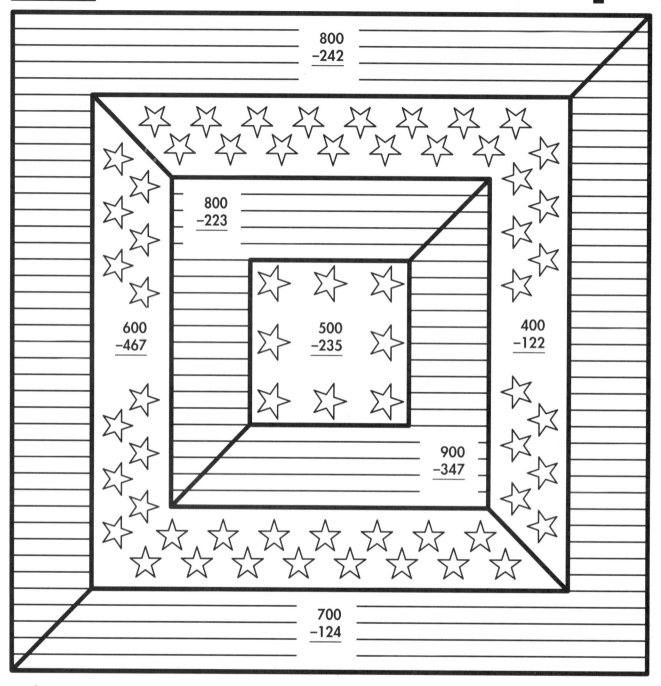

800
−242

800
−223

600
−467

500
−235

400
−122

900
−347

700
−124

Color:
>400 = red
<300 = blue

This design honored the home of our President.

C Write the names of at least four Presidents on the back of this sheet of paper.

Peony

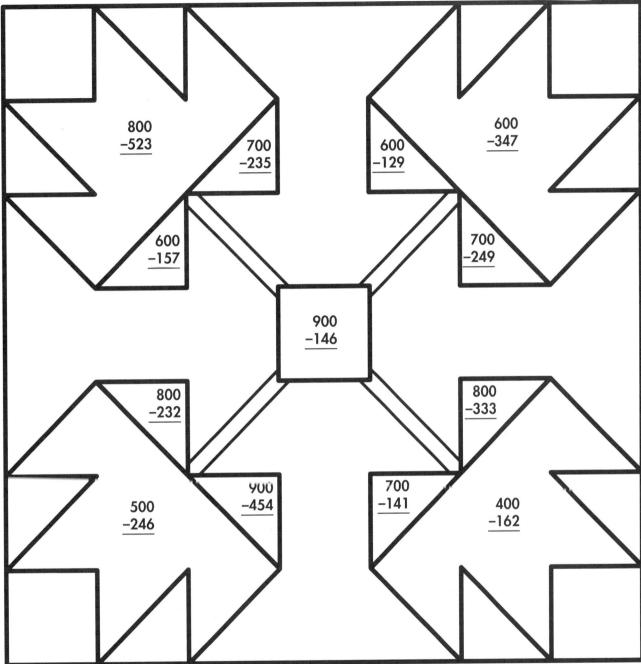

800
−523

700
−235

600
−347

600
−129

600
−157

700
−249

900
−146

800
−232

800
−333

500
−246

900
−454

700
−141

400
−162

Color:

100–300 = pink

400–600 = green

700–900 = brown

Look for these flowers in the spring.
They are usually pink or white.

C On a separate sheet of paper, draw
four flowers and put math problems in
them for your neighbor to do.

Duck Paddle

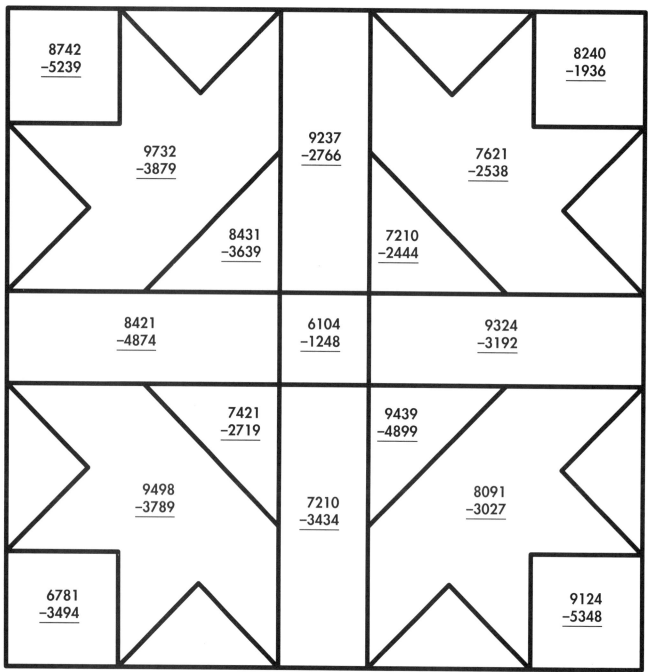

8742
−5239

8240
−1936

9732
−3879

9237
−2766

7621
−2538

8431
−3639

7210
−2444

8421
−4874

6104
−1248

9324
−3192

7421
−2719

9439
−4899

9498
−3789

7210
−3434

8091
−3027

6781
−3494

9124
−5348

If the thousands place is:
3—color yellow
4—color blue
5—color orange
6—color yellow

This picture does not resemble a duck, but use your imagination and you can almost see a duck's feet hidden in each square.

C Choose one problem from this page and write it on the back of this sheet of paper using words instead of numbers.

 # Double Z

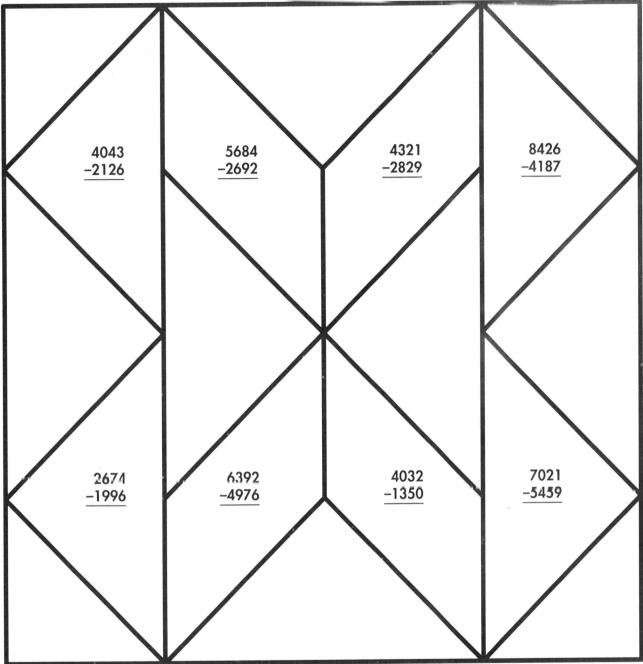

4043
−2126

5684
−2692

4321
−2829

8426
−4187

2674
−1996

6392
−4976

4032
−1350

7021
−5459

If answer has:
   9—color blue
   6—color yellow

Can you see at least two Z's in this picture?

_____

C On the back of this sheet of paper, write
   the numbers between these two numbers:
   7002 and 7031.

Star of LeMoyne

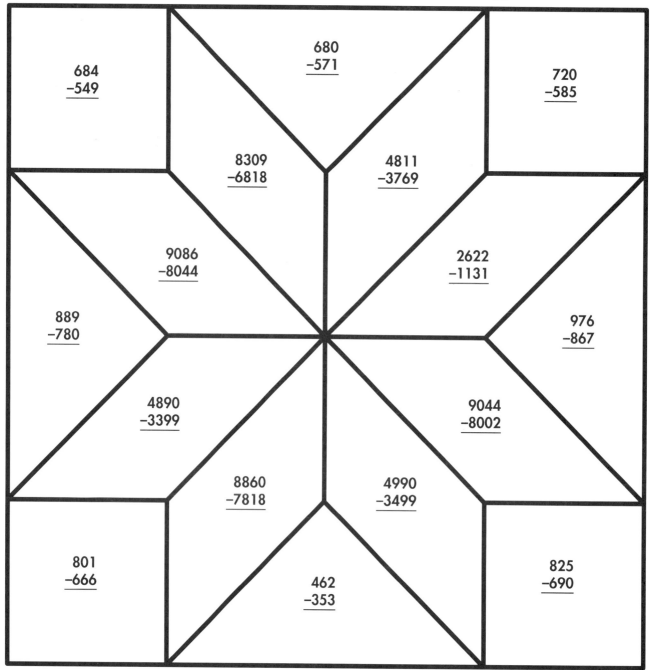

684
−549

680
−571

720
−585

8309
−6818

4811
−3769

9086
−8044

2622
−1131

889
−780

976
−867

4890
−3399

9044
−8002

8860
−7818

4990
−3499

801
−666

462
−353

825
−690

Color:
  135 = blue
  109 = green
  1042 = yellow
  1491 = orange

This was named for the LeMoyne Brothers.
They founded the city of New Orleans.

C On the back of this sheet of paper, make the
smallest and largest numbers from the given
numbers: 2, 9, 6, 8.

Lincoln's Platform

84 −48	90 −15

423
−179

82
−38

89
−14

862
−618

923
−787

990
−515

96
−38

769
−111

762
−287

60
−16

771
−635

790
−546

839
−364

937
−279

94
−36

100
− 25

98
−54

94
−50

823
−579

448
−312

82
−07

936
−461

92
−56

Color:

36 and 136 = red

44 and 244 = brown

58 and 658 = orange

75 and 475 = green

In the 1800s, it was the custom to present the new President with a quilt named for him. This was one person's gift quilt.

C On the back of this sheet of paper, make four different subtraction problems using these numbers: **46, 289, 192, 56.**

Symbol

Quilt Name _____

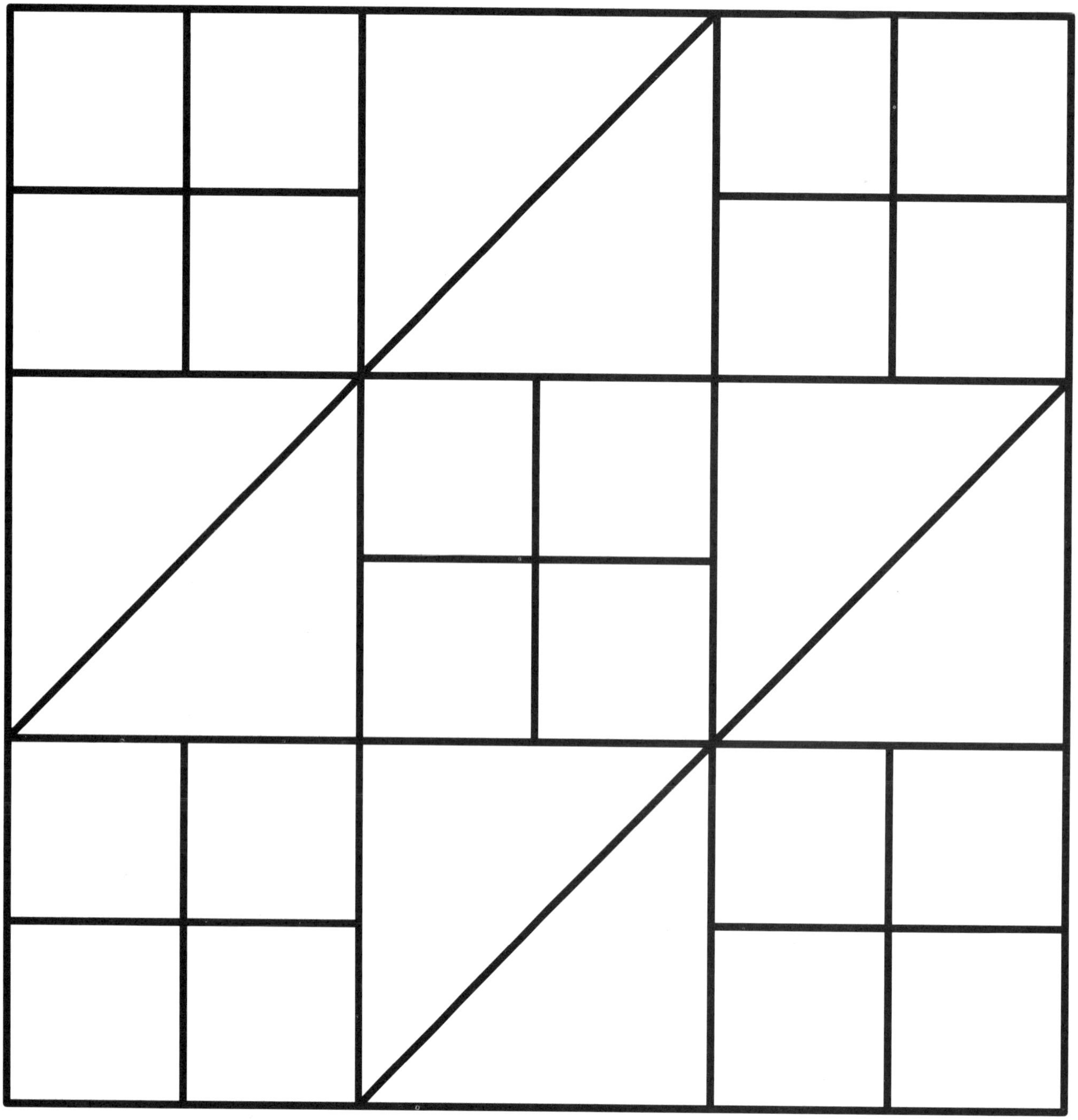

Color code:

This quilt pattern has two names. They are "Tail of Benjamin's Kite" and "Trail of the Covered Wagon." Select one of the names and make a color code to fit the design. Then make math facts to fit the color code.

Symbol

**Quilt
Name** _____

Color code:

Design a pattern for a quilt square on this grid. Base your design on the footprint shape of an animal you like. Name the design, and color it using colors that best illustrate its meaning. On the back of this sheet of paper write a short story about the animal.

**Quilt
Name** _____

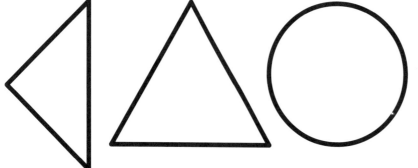

Cut out the shapes on the left to use as patterns. Trace them in a design in this square. Color the design any way you want. Name your pattern and draw a symbol for it.

Resources

Lenice Ingram Bacon: *Quilting*

Dolores A. Hinson: *A Quilter's Companion*

Dolores A. Hinson: *Quilting Manual*

Marguerite Ickis: *The Standard Book of Quilt-Making and Collecting*

Bonnie Leman: *Quick and Easy Quilting*

Maggie Malone: *One Hundred Fifteen Classic American Patchwork Quilt Patterns*

Ruby Mckim: *One Hundred and One Patchwork Patterns*